for Arthur

Bill Manning

THE RELENTLESS JEW

JESUS SPEAKS TODAY

BILL MANNING

Balboa Press books may be ordered through booksellers or by contacting:
Balboa Press
A Division of Hay House
1663 Liberty Drive
Bloomington, IN 47403
www.balboapress.com
1 (877) 407-4847

Printed in the United States of America.

ISBN: 978-1-4525-8920-6 (sc)
ISBN: 978-1-4525-8921-3 (hc)
ISBN: 978-1-4525-8922-0 (e)

Library of Congress Control Number: 2013923436

Balboa Press rev. date: 1/14/2014

ACKNOWLEDGEMENTS

I would like to thank Connie Manning, Sharon and Darel Ellert for their support and understanding during the three years it has taken to write this book… Also to my daughter Beth Becker for her ongoing encouragement and belief in me and the use of their cottage where I found the peace and quiet I needed. To my fried Wally Ziezig for her editing and invaluable contribution. Thank you all so very much.

PROLOGUE

Most who believe there is a God, have asked for help during difficult times. A few have heard God asking themselves for help. On occasions such as this the future of a country may be changed but more often a single life takes on a new course. There is constant communication between God and each person on this planet. Yet in the rush of daily living many messages are lost and an opportunity is missed. Those who have heard and accepted their task, may get the call again. The call may come during sleep, or as an idea.

It was just such a voice that prompted this book. Sit down and write what you will know…

So I wrote

Please note that as the words of Thomas were channeled, they were not edited or altered in any fashion.

Chapter One

This is the story of my family. Some of it told to me as I sat by the knee of my mother or from my father as we dined. Later much from my brother and the rest… well I just lived it.

Joseph walked along a dusty hot pathway, wiping sweat from his brow with his sleeve. It had been a long hot walk. A very impatient donkey walked by his side. The animal, resentful, tired, and thirsty was pulling a cart loaded with the mans tools of his trade. When they passed others it was not uncommon for them to call out a greeting. "Hello Joseph.". If the face of the man was not immediately familiar they knew the cart. It belonged to Joseph of Bethlehem. "Need a new well,, add a room, or even give good advice. Joseph is your man." His fame as a person who could just about fix anything, including entertaining at your wedding was legendary. Not only because of his all around skill but his congeniality and common sense made him good company. Joseph liked people and they liked him. He was understanding and compassionate, but his cart was distinctive. You could tell it a long way off by the large array of tools piled haphazardly upon it, covered here and there by white lime dust giving it a personality of its own. Joseph used lime to coat houses as his predecessors had in years gone by.

The bearded man strode on whistling through his front teeth, a happy man, characteristically friendly and a good man to know. His four legged friend accompanied the tuneless sounds of his master with the occasional bray

The day was hot for for late autumn and the roadway was dusty. The dryness for weeks had made people anxious and irritable none more so than the donkey. Joseph understood and talked softly in its ear, knowing the animal was hot and very thirsty, probably hungry too. Anyone who depended on a donkey in their work paid attention to their four-legged companions. It is well known donkeys will sit down in the middle of the road and refuse to move. Joseph could end up pulling the cart himself, he thought. A smile creased his good natured face as the notion moved across his mind. He was thirsty himself. She (the donkey) had not been fed since dawn and now it was past mid afternoon. It takes so little to raise the ire of any donkey at the best of times and Geddy (the donkey's name) being an strong example to this rather than an exception. "We will be there soon old girl," he said while at the same time rubbing the beast's mane and noticing the dust he created just with the movement of his hand.

"We are going to our next job and we'll be there awhile so you can take it easy and get lots of rest. You'll get a drink of good well water and sweet grass to eat. You can sit in the shade of an olive tree." Joseph could picture Geddy sitting on her haunches like a dog refusing to budge as she had done before and the memory caused him to chuckle. A good friend and in a manner of speaking a business partner, a companion for many years. The two travelled together from one village to another, fixing, building, and digging wells. They were welcome guests in an area that covered a large part of Canaan. Joseph was also known far and wide for his entertaining stories and good humour. The knowledge of his expertise and good company was passed from family to family he was seldom without a job.

They were just entering Nazareth as he spoke to Geddy. This was their destination, coming from Bethlehem, just about seven miles back. Joseph had stopped to fix a doorway on the way or they would have been there sooner. "I am to look for a white house that has had many additions and is about to get another," he mused aloud. "White house," he chuckled, "all the houses are white, I could use a better clue than that.

A man named Jacob wants me to build a rooftop room for a daughter he hopes to wed to someone not yet on the scene," Joseph snickered at his own humour as he talked on to the beast of burden. The donkey lifted its ears and let out a moaning sound every little while. Whether in complaint or possibly just to be sociable Joseph appreciated the fact Geddy was at least listening.

"Look Geddy," Joseph said, pointing to a house that seemed to fit the description, look at all the additions. This could be it. "We need to find a man called Jacob". A snort from the donkey indicated no more or less interest other than its about time. As he spoke a short, round, man appeared at the front door the house in question. He called out a greeting of surprise. "Hello and welcome! You must be the carpenter I had asked Elias to send my way. I did not expect you for another week, but I am glad to see you my friend." As was the custom he was dressed all in white to help ward off the hot sun, just as also was the carpenter. Jacob ambled out to the road to greet the traveller.

"And I guess with that remark you must be Jacob. Joseph grinned back. I am here early because a well I was to dig has been put off indefinitely. And speaking of wells, my four footed friend would like to get to one. She is old, tired, and thirsty. I guess hungry as well." "Jacob smiled reached out and patted the donkey who looked back at him with a cynical glare. He led the travellers around the back of the house where there was a well and a barn. "We keep our animals in here with the exception of the sheep of course. Give her a drink, the well is there. Help yourself to water and inside the barn is all the food your donkey will need. Why don't you unhitch the cart and tend to your beast while I call Ethel my wife, and my daughter Mary." Both will be delighted to see you we get so few visitors. They are out in the orchard pruning trees but will be glad of a break in their labours.

Jacob departed then and Joseph was left to tend to Geddy. When he had taken his donkey into the barn and given himself some cool water he found a bench in the shade and sat down. Talking to himself once again he commented on the well, which looked like it was as old as the house. "The well needs work, the house needs work, that with the room they wish built I can see we will be here for sometime."

After what seemed like a long wait he heard voices approaching and soon was rewarded as two women followed by Jacob came though the trees. "Joseph, meet my wife Ethel and my daughter Mary." The elder of the two women came forward and greeted

Joseph with friendly smile. Joseph extended both hands to her in a warm greeting. To maintain proper decorum and not offend his host, Joseph paid not the slightest mind to the young girl who was obviously the daughter, although it took all of his inner strength as Mary was indeed very beautiful. The daughter, Mary, stood back shyly with eyes cast down, as was proper, and adjusting her shawl a little closer to her face. At last Jacob said, "And this is this is my last unwed daughter, Mary. The girls face turned tomato red until Joseph's aplomb turned the embarrassing situation into a happy occasion by saying, Jacob, you are lucky to have had her company this long. Count your blessings." And with this he stepped forward and took both of her hands in his and said, "Mary, it must be for you I am going to build a room on the roof." Jacob quickly interrupted and said, "Let us have some food and then I will show you what it is we want. Yes the room is for my daughter Mary. Ours is a large family and we have built additions to this house for generations and now we will need to go up rather than out."

"That was the day Joseph met my mother, he immediately fell in love with her and she with him. They often shared the memory of their first meeting with each other in later times. True they did not know it was love in the beginning, but during the three months father worked at the household their love for each other was forged. In later years as the family grew both mother and father recounted that moment with all of us children as we sat together. Joseph was her first and only love she would relate, always with the warm look on her face I loved to see. She was thirteen years old and ready for marriage, that age being the custom in our land and although father was many years her senior, his maturity and strength drew her to him. On his part her delightful, happy, personality matched his own. Mother was considerably more mature and serious than her young age would suggest. She was ready and capable to become a wife. I never believed differently, God had a hand in there meeting.

Weeks later as Mary climbed the new stairs on the outside of the building as she would do every day, she marvelled at the smoothness of the new wood as well as its smell. She trailed her fingers along the railing and told herself she just wanted to watch this man at his work. She admitted to herself that she admired the confidence he displayed on the job. She saw him as a person who could be relied on in any situation. Here was a strong man whose character spoke for itself. The fact he was older never crossed her mind, she assured us later. It was easy for my brother and I to see her as having been mature at thirteen. She ruled the family and my brother being the outspoken person he was learned the hard way. She told us of their many conversations discussing their beliefs and hopes for the future. Mother wanted a large family one that would be steeped in the Jewish faith. Father wanted that too and it was then he told her he was married with two children. Mary was quickly assured by him this was not a problem. The two of them together could deal with it. My grandfather often said they were born for each other.

Joseph had an easy way of talking and Mary loved to listen, he was a storyteller. To a young girl who had never left Nazareth he appeared to be a man of the world, mature, confident, and reliable. She was in love, she may not have known it at the moment, but she was in love for the first and last time of her life.

As the days passed their fondness grew each day. Mother found herself visiting the roof to spend time with this amazing man. He was competent, strong in his opinions certainly, but fair, compassionate, and very thoughtful. She knew she was in love and knew instinctively he returned that love. Mother risked the biting tongue of her mother when she neglected her work on the farm, but her instincts drove her to be with this man every moment she could.

There was no doubt in their minds they were destined to be together. They soon turned to talk of their marriage and his existing marriage, which our father again hastened to assure her. "This will not be a problem for you, your family or the entire community. Marriages can be ended easily with the return of the dowry to the bride's parents and of my intentions in writing, plus the aid of a rabbi."

As Mother dreamed of the future she sensed this was to be a marriage of destiny; she told him about dreams she had, and he shared her dreams, they were so similar. They knew their time together would be short because of the nature of his work so they made the most of what time they had. It was going to be difficult for Mother to see him leave Nazareth and go off to work but she knew this was what he did and told him she understood as they held each other close. And so it was on a clear cold starry night in Tishri 1 (January) that in the light of a full moon, up on the roof Mary conceived.

Chapter Two

When Mary discovered she was pregnant she knew she must tell her parents and while she had already shared the knowledge of there intentions to marry, the pregnancy must be discussed. Grandfather and Grandmother knew of his marriage and had many discussions on the increasing involvement they had witnessed between the young couple. Because divorce at that time was not uncommon and easily accomplished they had little worry. But action on their part had to be taken soon, so they immediately announced the betrothal of their daughter to Joseph of Bethlehem.

Father was away for six months and by the time he arrived back in Nazareth Mary was large with child and her condition was no secret in this little town. Unfortunately and as expected in this tiny community of Nazareth talk of the pregnancy spread like wildfire and paternity was suspicious. The subject of much speculation. While it was not unusual for a girl to be pregnant before marriage if the father was a Jew. Most of the villagers put on their best neighborly smiles for the sake of mother's parents, Jacob and Ethel. But behind closed doors gossip raged rampant. Father was far away and Roman soldiers were stationed nearby adding fuel to the fire, many thought the worst. There was much whispering in this small community and finger pointing. Our mother was seen in the eyes of the village to have lain with a Roman soldier, and despite Joseph declaring the child as his, this baby was already labeled a "mamzer" (bastard or outcast). Despite this, the young couple were determined more than ever to marry.

Father had two children in his former marriage named James and Jude and with the dissolution of that marriage they would come with him to Nazareth. Thus he would divorce his present wife and move to the home of Mary bringing his sons with him. It was the custom that the male children remain with the father. As I mentioned divorce at that period of time was easy, Joseph merely told his wife they were divorced, issued a certificate, returned the dowry to her parents and it was done. Then Mary and Joseph were wed in Nazareth. That was how it worked, it was the custom and it was their wish.

Thus he left his home in Bethlehem taking with him his sons James and Jude and walked the seven miles to his new home in Nazareth to begin his new life and await the baby. Mother knew her child would be a boy, she just knew it, more like felt it. However neither she nor her husband nor the soon- to- be grandparents, expected twin boys. The second baby boy (me) was certainly going to be a surprise for everyone.

Because of the mood of the people in Nazareth it was felt things would work better if they travelled to Bethlehem for the birth and later the circumcision ceremony which was to follow. Mother knew this ceremony would assure her child a place in the community of Israel. The bond of blood united all Jews, even those of the mamzer caste. They set off on foot to walk the seven miles with Mary riding part of the way on a donkey. Mary's mother, Ethyl, accompanied this little procession, leaving James and Jude at home in Nazareth.

On a crisp, clear October twenty third at midnight,My brother and I made our entrance to the world. My parents knew what they would call this male child when he came screaming and kicking into the world. Baby Jesus was being held by the proud father, just as grandmother Ethyl, exclaimed loudly, "Look. There is another about to come." At this point I made my grand entrance into this world. According to my mother we were identical from the start. I was named Thomas, or Tum. Throughout our lives Jesus and I looked so much alike we were often mistaken for each other.

Our parents held their two boys ready to have the covenant with Israel marked into their flesh. The circumcision ceremony was to be completed by a highly respected elder who left with the blood and foreskin immediately afterward to bury them. These were considered unclean and the person who performed the operation was considered to be unclean until he had finished and washed. After the twin birth and circumcision ceremony we all traveled back to Nazareth to live together as a larger family than had first been expected. The first born son was named David Jesus and I as the second born we called Didymos Judas Thomas, one name-meaning twin in our Aramaic language and the other twin in Hebrew.

Chapter Three

Back in Nazareth mother and father discovered traveling to Bethlehem for the birth of their sons did not alter how the people here viewed their new born. We were mamzer children of suspected paternity, and it stuck. Such men and women lived in a caste apart, unable to marry within the established bloodlines of Israel. That would be more crucial to Jesus in later years than me. However we would be excluded from the religious life of our community. As he grew older this went a long way in shaping the thinking and attitude of my brother. The town still believed mother had lain with a Roman soldier and that was unforgivable. Jesus and I often talked about the exclusion we lived with; he felt a great degree of bitterness toward the priests and rabbis, as for me I just did not care.

From the time he was old enough to understand Jesus felt the hostility of the community. There is little doubt that he was plagued be that exclusion and labeling. Being on the receiving end of the side-glance stares, the snippets of gossip, the giggling behind cupped hands and being shut out of mainstream society had a great impact on Jesus in shaping a need for him to seek God as his father. Our own father Joseph observing the stares, the knowing, and the separation from the population, I am sure this was a factor in shaping need for Jesus to seek God as his father. Our father Joseph was not demonstrative with his affection toward the boys as he was to his daughters. He expected us to grow up and quickly and mimic men. If you are wondering why I say daughters, yes there were girls born into our family later.

My brother Jesus challenged authority early in life. He was quick to see the unfairness upheld by the gossip mongers in the community. We both quickly learned all was not fair in the world. Jesus became rebellious toward the priests and elders in the community. We were not allowed to attend religious ceremonies, not even when our father died. We were twelve then and this was another blow to my brother. He often told me that someday he would right the many wrongs of those with narrow minds who divided people by rules. In the meantime we were a close family, the foundation of which was love. Joseph our father was the head and the leader and now he was gone. We had lost our anchor and rock.

I remember my father so well. His voice could be soft and encouraging or when angry low and menacing. His mind was sharp when planning buildings or fixing them. His love for my mother and us was the power that kept him going.

Looking back I still see him, not tall, stocky, well built and born with long arms and big hands. Being slightly bow legged caused him to walk with a rolling gate. His hair and beard was black, his eyebrows stood out so far from his face they often-collected dust and shavings from the wood he worked with. He was a hairy man. It covered his arms, legs, chest, and even down his back. We children would laugh and call him monkey man. He loved it and would chase us with a little hopping motion, allowing his arms to hang at his sides while his hands opened and closed. He was affectionate and playful with all of his children when they were little but as we matured, so did he, he took on a more reserved nature.

During playtime I would often look to see Jesus standing off to the side by himself. It would often cross my mind wondering what he was thinking. If father had trouble showing affection, I noticed Jesus did also. Strange really when I look back and see how he could love all the entire world, but then God had not worked on him yet.

Jesus was compassionate and loving with mother who when we were little would hold both us boys on her knee and tell us stories of our Jewish history. Mother was the root of love. She loved everybody and everything. Jesus adored her and wanted to hear as much about our ancestors as he could. There was such a strong need to know as much as he could about our Jewish background. Later it would be the unfairness he saw in our religious teachers whose presentations clashed with stories of Moses and King David and the building of the temple. We learned how and why an earlier temple had been torn down and ravaged. Father seldom told us much about his ancestry other than his lineage back to King David.

Mother was short, round, and beautiful. I adored her. I can still feel her touch and remember the scent of her body as Jesus and I sat on her knee. While I loved being cuddled, Jesus would squirm to get down unless he was on her knee alone. It seemed he wanted all her attention, his very own cuddle time, She had large brown eyes that always seemed to be smiling. Mother was love. Everyone loved her and delighted in her company, by that I mean the townspeople as well as our family. She was the favorite of her father who was always bringing her little gifts. Mother loved God with a passion. She would often raise her eyes to the sky when picking a fruit from a tree and smiling would mouth thank you. We were taught always to be grateful not only to God, but to each other. "We have such a nice family my children, so we should thank God often."

Mother never believed God was a vengeful God, but forgiving and loving. She believed God knew humans made mistakes and would be happy to forgive us when we sincerely asked. God was tolerant, she would say, but don't overdo it." She passed on to us the history that it was important we should know, from Abraham to King Solomon and she did this over and over again so we would never forget it. "Galilean Jews were indentured but not defeated," mother told us. "We burn with pride in a living memory of ourselves as the people of Israel who are descended from the patriarch Jacob, grandson of Abraham. We have tilled this soil and called the land ours for more than a thousand years fighting war after war, enduring defeat, genocide, and exile at the hands of foreigners. Our identity as Jews is bound up in the land and the covenant that made this land ours. This covenant is our last defense against Rome and our strongest."

Jesus would sit and listen to her every word. His mind was like a sponge soaking up every bit to be stored forever. It was necessary for us to learn our history and keep it in our minds. Since it would not be passed on in the written words because after all who could read them? Thus we must memorize them.

James was learning to read and write, but for the rest of the family this targum was our way to pass down our history. That is what made us Jews and in our minds this made us different. These special moments with mother were to live with Jesus and strengthen his Jewish beliefs for years to come.

James was big brother whom we all looked up to as he was expected to become a teacher and priest. For this reason he was sent out to learn to read and write. He was also excused from helping father in his work. James was taller than the rest of us and walked with long strides. He seemed to be constantly in a hurry. He wore his hair long and compared to fathers black, James hair was a soft brown. When father passed away James took over as head of the house. He was an impatient man and often had trouble keeping this irascibility in check especially with Jesus who was also impatient. It was assumed he would eventually move to Jerusalem to work in the Temple.

CHAPTER FOUR

Jude the second son of Joseph was introverted, said little, thought a lot and listened even more. You never knew what was going on in his head. Some thought him to be a little slow. He was not; just careful and cautious, a very sensitive human being. There was definitely was nothing wrong with his head. When he sat quietly without speaking mother would often say, "What are you thinking about Jude?" He would look up at her with a soft little smile on his face and shyly say, "lots of things." He could neither read or write, but he created poetry, which he recited and sang at family gatherings. James was later to put them in writing. Jude was a compassionate youth whose eyes would fill with tears at the slightest provocation, he was tender, emotional, just a fountain of love. He was a natural farmer never to become a carpenter, but he would pick up a newborn lamb and see God in the creature. Every one loved Jude and he loved everyone and every thing. This earth we live on belongs to God he would say we are but tenants. He would go on to add: "Treat this land we live on with respect and it will provide." If one could not love Jude, no love lived in that heart.

Mother had four more children after Jesus and I. There was Ruth who was born with a deformity on her upper lip. She was father‘s favorite child. The love he held for her shone in his eyes every time he picked her up. When he would come back from a long trip the first thing he did upon entering the house was to seek out Ruth. Then there was Simon who died quite young and two more girls who were born frail and also died young. These last two became the charge of Jude who was like a second mother to them. When he was working on the fruit trees they could be found with their brother Jude. When they died Jude wept and grieved for days.

Because Jesus and I were rejected by the community, James took on the task of teaching us. While Jesus was anxious to learn he was also a difficult student. He would not accept anything verbatim. He needed to take it apart and put it together again until he understood it. Jesus might say, “I cannot believe that came from God, it is not something God would say.” James would often become frustrated and tell Jesus he does not know what God would do and not do he must accept what he is taught. Jesus responded by saying that he did know God. The arguments never ended. Jesus told me he needed a new teacher. Sometimes Jesus would say I do not say it is wrong, but I challenge the interpretation. Jesus seemed driven to learn and would go out in the dark and under the stars and pray to God for a proper teacher.

James talked about the temple in Jerusalem saying it is where God lives. Jesus said God lives everywhere. Wait until you get there young man James would say there is a room called the holiest of the holies which is God's own room. Just see what you have to say when you are there. As it turned out that day was not far away. We were chosen as one of the families to be allowed to go to Jerusalem.

Chapter Five

Jerusalem, the Temple, and the Holy of the Holies. This is where God's own room is to be found. Miracle of miracles, we were going! Adding to our excitement we would arrive in time for the Day of Atonement and the Festival of Sukkoth, or Tabernacles. In our village only a few families were allowed to leave at one time. The elders gave their permission for us to travel along with the rest of those from our village who had been chosen. The selection of only a few families was necessary because in the fall of the year people were needed to harvest the crops. We worked as a community and what we grew must feed us for a year. Thus the reason for family selection.

It was arranged Jude would stay to look after the livestock and the rest of the family. Actually it was his preference to remain at home. This was not a hardship for our brother. He was the dreamer, the composer the one who lived in his own mind. The thought of the travel and the crowds only frightened him. Ruth also preferred to stay at home; she was sensitive because of her face and of course she loved Jude so dearly and wanted to be with him. She could never bear to mix with strangers. The other two girls were not well enough to travel. Mother would only leave knowing

Jude would be back home and taking care. As I said before he was like a mother to the children.

To say we were excited was an understatement. Jesus and I were exuberant. We piled on all the clothes we could wear. This was because we could not carry extra bundles; the alternative was to wear them. We started off as a large group, but on the road the families eventually separated, each maintaining their own pace or with a plan of their own. Our little group wanted to push ahead. We would camp at the side of the road rather than stop at an inn. The nights were cool and the extra clothing not only was welcome, it was a must. From our home it was a five-day walk to Jerusalem at best. We would cross the highlands of Galilee which seemed almost familiar because father often worked in these parts and and would come home talking about the countryside in great detail. In some way it just seemed we already had a preview of this part of the world. Most families brought along some livestock which would be sold in Hammath. In this way people have some money to buy a goat at the temple that we would later sacrifice and also cover travel expenses. It might seem odd to bring an animal and selling it only to buy one later at the temple. To bring our own as far as the temple would anger the priests and make them hostile. Of course we wanted to avoid that. The other side of the coin was that selling our own animal freed us from the very real possibility that a wild beast might come and steal ours… Mother thought it was a good trade. The priests make money selling us sacrificial animals and we had one less problem on the way to the temple to deal with. Hammath was on ancient trade route and the people here used currency in their daily lives. Back in Nazareth we used a barter system it was very unlikely we would ever have actual money in our possession. We exchanged goods or services, meat, grain, or even clothing. The citizens of Nazareth would never think of looking for profit either. My fourteen year old brother Jesus could not accept the concept of commercialism by those whose duty it was to preach God's word. He saw it as pure greed. Remember we lived in a very small part of the world. Yet many years later Jesus still viewed currency with great suspicion,

From Hammath it was downhill and into the wilderness of the hostile Jordan Valley where wild animals lived in abundance. Despite this we camped here for our first night, not wishing to use our paltry finances to rent a room in town. We knew there was risk here because of the wild animals and but even more so there was the very real danger of robbers. It would be necessary for one person to remain awake to keep watch while the rest slept. The farther south we travelled the imperative for keeping guard increased. Near the end of the journey we reached an area where the river widened and formed little pools where we could wash up. We were grateful for this opportunity to rid ourselves of the dust of the road. Our destination was the town of Bethany where mother had two older aunts Miriam and Martha and we wished to arrive there as clean as possible; as was only good manners.

It was with mixed feelings that Jesus and I found ourselves standing outside this strange door. However Miriam and Martha were so glad to see us and quickly made up a welcoming meal. How could we know that about fifteen years later Jesus would stay with them again? It is a good thing we did not know what the next decade and a half had in store for the family, especially Jesus.

Tabernacle celebration was a family solidarity occasion and out gathering was a joyous one. They knew a year in advance that we were coming and they went to great lengths to prepare a wonderful welcome. They cooked a spring lamb which was a delicacy saved for very special visitors. The council in Nazareth chose the attendees a year in advance and informed our family that we were among the chosen. Thus we were able to let Martha and Miriam know many months before our impending visit, giving them a deal of time to prepare.

Their house seemed large compared to ours back home in spite of all the extensions added to our house, or maybe because of them. Also their house sat on a busy street often filled with people. As I looked out I pulled Jesus to the doorway and whispered to him, "Where are their fields and livestock? Did you see the carpets on the floor? They must be wealthy." Jesus frowned and said he could not understand why the Holy One would bestow so much wealth on people who did not care for fields or livestock. We were farmers and once again had a different perspective and possibly saw things through naive eyes.

The next morning James set out to buy a goat for sacrifice. He walked to Jerusalem where there would be vendors close to the Temple. He went to an area near the north gate, close by the Roman fortress. James shuddered as he passed it. Like all of us the spectre of Rome was a constant and frightening reality. Although he was more experienced than the rest of the family in dealing with merchants, he was not comfortable in their company because it required bargaining and haggling. He tried to cover up his insecurity with a thin veil of haughtiness. James regaled us with side-splitting laughter when he replayed his haggling prowess later. Jesus and I sat and giggled.

It was the hope of James that one day he would be accepted by the high priest to become part of the temple staff. So while he was bargaining with the merchant priests he also attempted to show his sophistication and appear as though he belonged.

James was a very serious person. It was always important to him to do the right thing. He would look for an animal that would cost the least, but also please God. Never-the-less it was easy for vendors to see him as being from a small farming community and overcharge him. James did not wish to deprive God of a good sacrifice, but he believed God would know we were not wealthy and understand his need to be thrifty.

Having decided on a goat he took it directly to the Temple to be inspected by the priests who would then decide on whether the animal was of suitable quality for offerings of the day. The ever insistent Jesus argued when you buy from one priest why would a second priest need to inspect and approve it if the seller was also a priest. Who was honest? Who was dishonest? My suspicious brother. It was also customary to leave some currency for the priests along with the offering. In today's world you would call it a tip. However James was not inclined to do so and after leaving the goat walked quickly away from the north gate never looking back. The family planned to present the remaining offerings of grain and wine personally. James headed to the south gate where it was arranged that he would meet the rest of the family as well as some of the town's people. He would have liked to hand over the animal at the point of sacrifice so the offering would be known to come from our family. But the priests were far too busy for that to allow for that to happen. "Surely God would know it was from us," Jesus snapped, "Providing of course our God agrees with the concept of sacrifice"

Later that day when we met James at the south end of the temple, our excitement had mounted to fever pitch. None of us would ever forget these next two days. Jesus and I were practically jumping. With the exception of James the family had never been this far away from home and here we were in Jerusalem, which to us was the centre of the world. The site of this building transfixed us, it gleamed white in the sun and the stonework seemed to sparkle as the walls reached up almost to the heavens. The sun glinted off the gilt of the enormous Sanctuary, which was said to be the largest building in the world.

Mother told us that in the room called the Holy of the Holies, no human ever entered, except the High Priest and that was only once a year on the Day of Atonement and this was the Day of Atonement. We were so blessed. Here is where God lived.

We had been thinking of nothing else and could not wait to see this special part of the temple. I'm certain that if Jesus had had the opportunity he would have entered this Holy of Holies on his own -- not as a sacrilege-- but because of his closeness to Abba, the Father. This was not something anyone else would or could fully understand. Jesus felt so comfortable with God his closeness was like family. Where others would fall to the ground and avoid looking at the face of God; Jesus would drink in His presence and send his love with his eyes. My brother was different, I felt this from early in our lives. I can only add, this is a positive difference.

Of course Jesus knew it would have been impossible to enter this most sacred realm. I only mentioned this because of the comfort my brother felt where God was concerned. Moreover the room was well guarded. Anyone trying to enter would have been executed. As Roman soldiers nor anyone not Jewish were not allowed inside the temple there were Jewish guards dressed very much like Roman soldiers who stood guard. This decree of dress code by the high priest was acceptable even preferred both by the son of Herod and Pilate, but despised by the Jewish population.

Sacrificial offerings were considered to be the absolute gift one could give to God, but Jesus even at his young age had his doubts as I told you before. He absolutely opposed taking food that could feed hungry people and burning it on a fire where it would do no good to anybody and calling it a sacrifice to God. How could God benefit from this? It was commons knowledge that the sacrificial flesh would later be sold, for a profit or even worse –to non Jews, even Romans. My brother Jesus was opinionated of that there was no doubt, but when I stopped to consider his point of view it made sense to me. He believed a person should talk to God in prayer often, do it with feeling and love, openness and understanding, like you would a close friend. This type of sincere devotion would connect you to oneness with the Almighty. I knew what my brother was thinking I guess I always did.

However if the meat from the sacrifice were made available to the poor and homeless it would make sense. But when non-Jews could buy it and the proceeds go to the already wealthy, my brother strenuously objected. Jesus would later undergo many more changes in his own philosophy regarding his interpretation of, the traditional teachings, all of which only widened the chasm between him and the Jewish leaders. However, there was never any doubt that Jesus considered himself to be a good Jew.

To make our way we climbed up the hill towards the temple itself, which was on high. As we looked ahead to the edifice itself I could not help but recall what Mother had told us about this structure. What we were looking at was actually the second Temple on this very spot. King Solomon the son of our beloved King David built the first temple, which had been a dream of his father David. It involved huge amounts of building materials and funds for the construction. It was said to be the temple of temples built for the glorification of God. The temple was set on the summit of Mount Mariah on the east side of Jerusalem and the very site where Abraham, the father of our faith, offered his son Isaac up as a sacrifice to God.

This monument to the love of God was not to last. King Nebochadanaazzar of Babylon looted it and took all of the valuables back to Babylon. Later he ordered it destroyed. It was also said he had ordered his soldiers to take any written evidence that the building had even existed. However the desolate rubble and ruin had lain there for years as evidence of this crime. Our mother told us this story many times so we would never forget it. No Jew should. She always told it the same way, word for word as it had been told to her. Jesus always listened with rapt attention and used to asked many questions. He could and would tell this exactly the same way to others. The destruction of this temple became a rallying force for all our people. This act of treachery would be remembered by Jews forever.

The second temple was built in exactly the same place by exiles, (our people) which had escaped or been released by the Babylonians. The foundation had been laid about five hundred years before our time and what little was left of the building had been decaying and damaged by hostile soldiers when King Herod the great took the throne.

King Herod The Great wanted to gain favour with our people and offered to rebuild and restore this temple. His offer was met with great rejoicing and support. If nothing else Herod was lavish in his appointments and completed the main section in about ten years. There was still much to be done when we arrived, but it was glorious to all of us from Nazareth. Herod could not be anything but Herod. He wanted to play to every audience. For the Jews he built the temple, for Mark Anthony he placed a great eagle, the emblem of the Romans and for Tiberius he enlarged Jerusalem by extending the wall around the city. While the Jews loved the temple the eagle was an affront and the hatred toward Herod only increased.

King Herod died when we were about four years old and his grandson Herod Antipas succeeded him. Antipas was a Tetrarch meaning one quarter. His kingdom was Galilee, east bank and Perea. As the power was in transition, three men, all of them shepherds each gathered together armies of Jews to revolt against the Romans. One of them a man named Simon from the town of Perea fought courageously and came close to defeating the Roman army, but in the end was no match for the well- trained soldiers of Pilate. Finally he fell in battle dying in a stoney ravine where no plants grew or water found its way. His body was left unburied in this stone filled, dusty gulley as a reminder to all who would defy Rome's might. Three days after his death his followers claimed to have seen his spirit rise from his body. They proclaimed him as the Messiah saying his soul had risen from his dead body and was amongst them. They prophesied his spirit would lead them to freedom from the Roman invaders. Our young brother Simon was named after him.

CHAPTER SIX

As we grew close to this wonder of wonders, we strained our eyes to see ahead even though the Temple itself was far above us. The closer we got, the greater were the crowds gathering around us began to thicken. There were throngs of visitors from many different lands, wearing many different costumes. Who were they and where did they come from? We spoke in whispers even though no one could hear us. There had been nothing in our daily lives, no experience to compare with this or even to prepare us. We were filled with a blend of awe, excitement, and yes, even embarrassment. We felt like little people in a land of giants.

The blend of smoke and burnt meat filled our nostrils and made our eyes water from away down here. All of this fuelled the excitement that had been building for days. Some of the young worshippers who came from our village joined Jesus and me giggling at the way some of the women dressed. Our mother spoke sharply to us, telling both Jesus and I we must show respect.

It was important to be clean before heading up to the gates and into the presence of the Holy One. Before going in to the temple we needed to bathe. This was done in the pools at the foot of the

Temple Mount. To cleanse properly was done by immersion. We had already been climbing up from Siloam, passing masses of vendors selling almost anything one would want for themselves or last minute offerings. There were separate baths for men and woman and also Gentiles. Male youths were herded off with their mothers. It was amazing to see the system of canals and cisterns that brought the water to the baths, the construction was ingenious. How could anyone living in a little community such as Nazareth even grasp the enormity of this incredible edifice?

Finally it was time for us to set foot in the building itself. This was the realization of our dream, to actually be here in the house of God. Up until now this was something we had only heard about dreamed about. Our greatest hopes were about to be realized. Can you not imagine our excitement and pride at being Jews? We trembled, our legs felt weak, we continued to speak in whispers as we moved forward one step at a time. Our emotion left us both frightened and unbelieving. Were we worthy? We were about to visit God. I was dizzy with exhilaration, I know my twin brother was too.

Fighting to control our emotions we mounted the very wide stairs and climbed carefully. Because of the multitude climbing alongside us pushing and shoving a fall here would be hazardous. The height was dizzying. So many people from so many countries, Gentiles as well as Jews all were heading toward the gates above clamouring to reach the top.

The clothing of many of the women was unlike anything we had ever seen before all we could do is gape and wonder. Romans from afar all excited laughing and talking loudly, it seemed offensive to those like us from little country villages such as Nazareth. Some Jewish hucksters called out to Gentiles claiming they could take them throughout the Temple where no non-Jew was allowed, for a small fee of course. It was a lie, non- Jews entering the Temple would be put to death, but many accepted the offer only to be turned back before they entered the gate. This just was another example of the greed for money that had infiltrated this the home of the one and only God. It was not lost on Jesus. On the one hand was the divinity of the place and on the other was the overwhelming consumerism. That part of it was lost on me, but not on Jesus.

I felt the shudder that ran through my brother was viable to me as he looked at those who obviously would not be allowed to enter. Why are they here, this close to the gate? This is the house of God, why do they mock Him? Looking back on it later I saw how his love for God was mixed with his loathing of the use of this building as a market to garner money and was instrumental in shaping his convictions. In years to come a Jesus matured some of his views were moderated as you will learn later. While Jesus saw the temple as strictly for Jews, many years later he would say God is for all people.

Even though they bathed, Gentiles were not allowed into the Great Court. Armed Jewish soldiers barred the way. The interior courts were reserved for Israelite. Here the males and females separated if they had not already. A guide led us into the temple explaining as we went the features of the temple. We all felt the glory of God around us and trembled in awe. I grasped Jesus arm shaking it and asked him if he could not feel the presence of God.

He replied yes but God is also everywhere and we only feel like this because we have opened ourselves to Him. It is possible to feel God's closeness like this any time you wish. However I know he was as overwhelmed as I. Jesus was Jesus and I knew he felt as I was.

Walking through the enormous gates we could not see much as the staircase inside was windowless and the climb was the equivalent of four stories. The height itself was intimidating and scary, especially to me because I was afraid of heights. Where in all of Judea was there a building this large? There were torches burning along the way, but they did little to illuminate this expansive area.

Coming out of the dark into the sun as we left the stairway was a blow to the optic nerves and we had to cover our eyes for a moment. The dazzling display of sun on the gold and silver left us breathless. We were assigned to stay with our mother and go into the court for women. We found ourselves near the Sanctuary of white marble, called the Holy of Holies. Jesus and I had talked endlessly about this moment since we had left home, now we were actually here in this place we had only dreamed about. Our throats were dry and we spoke in raspy voices. Here was the ultimate moment of our lives and we were here.

I do not know if I can describe fully how it felt. Even Jesus, who had argued earlier that the closeness of God could be experienced equally anywhere, could not deny this moment, I tingled from my inner core to the outer most area of my skin. I could feel each hair on my arms, it was almost painful. My skin felt both hot and cold as it reacted to this unbelievable awe. I stood transfixed, afraid to breathe or even move. Was this fear, love, or panic? I was here in the presence of God. My eyes wanted to close but were afraid to miss something. From my toes to the hair on my head the sensation was that of living in another life or another body. This was God's home, God's essence. I dropped to my knees along with my brother as we held each others hand. We would never be the same again. We wept from sheer joy and the tears ran from our eyes to our mouths, the salt burning on cracked lips.

The inner court was a rough structure made of uncut stones, probably twenty or more feet high, and it contained the alter fire. This was nothing more than a pit of blazing logs surrounded by young priests throwing wine, corn and animals into this inferno. All around were ramps where the priests worked. Smoke, ashes, embers and blood were spread around everywhere. These priests were dressed in what might what might have been ornate robes but were now covered in blood and gore, peeled down to their naked waists, their sweaty backs glistening in the light of the crackling orange flames. In the background just out of sight the sacrificial animals bellowed in fear, knowing somehow that death was in the air, and soon it would be their turn. The celebratory symphony of sounds was completed by the popping and splashing of fat, the singe and stench of burning animal hair, and the sizzling and smoke of wine as it was poured into the flames mixed with that sound was the popping of fat and the sizzling of wine as it was poured into the flames. Our offering of wine and wheat was cast into this inferno and instantly disappeared. Our only acknowledgement was that our eyes burned and watered from the smoke, if we thought it bad down below, up here it was infernal.

Our lungs rebelled as we inhaled, but nothing could dispel the total incomprehension of the moment.

Jesus and I stared at all of this then we moved away from this frenzy and found ourselves back at the Sanctuary. We held still held hands in awe as we realized we were actually here, we who had been labelled mamzer, we who had not been allowed to attend our father's funeral, were here in God's presence. In the midst of all of this I felt God's love and I know Jesus did too. I did not know until then what 'one with God' truly meant, but my heart felt it. For I felt the rapture to be part of God himself at that very moment. But total understanding of that concept would be a long way off.

Because my head was a jumble of thoughts, my body numbed by the experience, I asked myself what was it I felt besides this numbness? Was it wonder at being a part of all this, did I feel insignificant? With these thoughts buzzing in my head I wandered alone around this huge building, Jesus having gone his own way. This place was not a synagogue nor was it the temple I had imagined it would be.

What was Jesus thinking? I turned to ask him and realized he was gone. I guess he might have been as confused as I was, I thought. So where was Jesus? I set out to find that brother of mine. Later, much later I learned he had wandered further away and mixed with the crowd. He sought a place where he could be quiet and think and pray, mostly pray. There was too much happening inside so he just went outside. That was no easy feat. Down the hill and away from all the merchants he wandered off to be alone. Finally away from all the turmoil he sat down under a fig tree and talked to God, here in this place of worship where God and greed worked side by side. This temple where he found true feelings of love, understanding, and compassion alongside avarice and thirst for power.

As he sat alone he called out, "I am sickened by the presence of Romans soldiers and tourists even outside. There are merchants here whose only business is to sell and prosper. This seems fundamentally wrong but maybe I just do not understand." All this Jesus said to God aloud while people walked by not even giving him a single glance. With hands together in front of his face he asked for understanding. "I need to learn so much and I will not learn it back home where there is nobody to teach me. I pray for guidance and promise I will do whatever it takes to become useful to you and all people."

Not until many years later, when Jesus and I were both men did he explain and share with me the moments of rapture, revulsion, shock and despair of this experience. For it was this night that Jesus left, disappeared from our lives and none of us would see him again for fifteen years.

Around the time Jesus decided to go on his walk about,the Emperor Augustus in far off Rome suddenly died and was replaced by Tiberius. As that great leader took office he could not guess more than fifteen years later the man Jesus would become such a threat to the high priest of the temple in Jerusalem and become a concern to himself back in Rome. The die was cast when Jesus began his real education on his personal journey.

So that night Jesus began walking. He walked and he walked until he was weary from walking. Completely drained, from over emotion, he found himself sitting under a tree where he closed his eyes and tried to think. At about the same time mother, James and myself decided our part in the sacrifice was over and our time here was done. We were ready to go back home. Mother turned to me and said, "Thomas, where is Jesus?" I replied, "I have been looking for him and have not found him. He had been with me constantly and now was is nowhere to be found. "Perhaps he's exploring each and every little corner and then some. You know how he has a penchant for discovery." I replied jokingly. Knowing his tendencies we were more annoyed than worried. So we searched everywhere, but my brother had totally disappeared. I was accustomed to look for him it was my task and in the past I always found him. This time was different. Mother was very concerned despite knowing Jesus tendency to do the unexpected. James came back from the male section where he had gone to look an informed us that he was not over there. Jesus had disappeared. Gone. We searched everywhere going over the places we had just looked. Jesus had vanished. Mother was now frantic. James was vexed. A deep gnawing feeling in the pit of my stomach had told me this might happen. Afraid to mention my thoughts to anyone I could no longer hold them back.

"Mother I think Jesus has left to find answers."

"What do you mean left Thomas?"

"I think he has gone off on his own to find the answers he has been unable to find anywhere." I offered. Mother could not accept this so after repeated searches produced no Jesus, we simply went back to the aunt's house in Bethany. They had not seen him either. Finally after days of waiting, not knowing what more we could do we reluctantly left for home, back to Nazareth. What else could we do? It was sometime on the trip home mother suddenly became very calm and knowing. A total changed swept come over her. God had came to mother in her sleep and told her all would be well. Her son was following his destiny. Even though she would not see him for years, there was a different look in her eyes. She had found peace. What it was she knew she never told anyone, but I believed our mother knew her son was safe, protected by God and would return home some day.

More than fourteen years would pass before we were reunited. At home life resumed its somewhat normal course. As for me I would go back to Nazareth and carry on my father's work as a carpenter. Later however my life took an unusual turn and I eventually drifted to the sea where I would become a builder of ships. I never married, travelled home whenever I could and watched over mother. I missed my brother, but strangely often felt his presence, perhaps he was thinking of me in those moments. When we were very young we would hold hands and tell each other we would be together always. Our lives had taken an unexpected turn. The twin brothers who looked so much alike, but were so different in aspirations took much different directions. Jesus at the age of fourteen would set off on a quest he could never have dreamed or expected would turn out as it did. That unshakeable faith he had in God was with him to guide and protect him of this there was no doubt. His life was to be shaped by the God he lived to serve. His plea to God for guidance with his promise to serve had begun.

CHAPTER SEVEN

Slowly and painfully Jesus opened his eyes. He was lying just off the trail still wrapped in his robe, and the damp chill of the early morning brought him quickly back to full consciousness. More than the discomfort of the hard ground, which had served as his bed for the night, he realized he was in pain. Shivering uncontrollably in the damp morning air, he struggled to to grasp his situation. He was both hot and cold at the same time. Now fear clutched him as he realized there something wrong with his left leg. The pain was intense. Confused and alarmed he struggled to sit up to have a closer look. He pulled up his robe and looked down at his leg and discovered that his calf was swollen to twice its normal size. It was discoloured and throbbed all the way up to his thigh. Then as he moved to sit up further and touch the leg a hand gently held back the move. This was the first time he became aware of a pair of large brown eyes looking at him with concern. The eyes belonged to a face which gradually focused into a body. Jesus saw two strangers sitting beside him, one holding his hand and another helping him to sit up.

A voice speaking to him in his own language was explaining something. What was it they were saying? "A viper has bitten you. You need treatment young master." The voice was soft and compassionate, reassuring. Jesus was startled, alarmed, and pulled himself back.

"Do not fear, I promise you are in good hands and above all safe." Jesus was strangely reassured. As his eyes focused on the source of this voice he now saw two men both dressed in strangely coloured robes. Orange? Or so they seemed. His thought his eyes must be playing tricks on him. It was later he was to learn they were Buddhist monks. Together these, men bent to help him up and aided him to a tent he had no recollection was there the night before. Assisting him into the tent they suggested he lay down on a carpet, which covered the floor. Gratefully the boy sank to the ground dizzy, in pain, confused, and feverish,. Jesus had some difficulty making sense out of all of this. Could this have been caused by the bite? It mattered not he just fell back surrendered to their ministrations and drifted into sleep.

Jesus had no idea how much time had passed when he woke up again. He watched as these two kind strangers worked on his leg. Seeing him back to consciousness, one of them offered him water, which he eagerly and gratefully gulped down. His mouth was parched, his tongue seemed swollen, even his vision was distorted. The two saviours promised to give him food after the treatment. He knew he needed that too and was grateful. Where was he, where were his mother and the rest of the family? Jesus struggled to recall how he got there. It was so difficult to focus on anything. He pushed his memory and slowly, bit-by-bit little pieces of the puzzle came back to him. Visions floated in and out of his mind. He recalled the temple and his frustration with the noise, the chatter, the smell, and his feelings about the commercialism. Then in frustration and futility, he fled. Was it all real? Did he do that? Then it all began to fade away and he slept once more. As he drifted in and out of sleep he moaned and twisted in agony until finally totally exhausted he slept again. While he slept the two men worked on his leg.

Much later he awoke again, suddenly recalling the two strange men who had helped him. Then as he became more cognitive his mind went back to yesterday, or was it yesterday? He recalled his flight from there to the streets followed by aimless wandering alone not knowing were he was going and being very hungry hungry. In desperation he even tried begging for food and received a slap for his effort. Humiliated and frightened he found himself out in the countryside and here. It all seemed so unreal. Again he needed to ask himself if he had actually done this. Left his family and wandered to this place, but, "where?" He tried to make some sense of his present predicament. Should he attempt to explain what he was doing here. He was not sure he himself knew. The smell of blood, the screaming animals, the shouting people, it all became a horror in his mind. He tried to block it with good thoughts of God and that other side of the temple where he and his brother prayed and felt the presence of God. Best to forget it and just lay back. The effort of remembering was actually very tiring.

Hi thoughts once more returned to his family, to his mother and what must they be thinking. He wondered what did they do?

when they could not find him? Jesus started to feel very guilty. Have I done the right thing? They must be worried. Everything seemed too much for this fourteen-year old fevered boy who had never been away from home. Once more opening his eyes he saw these kind men who had been helping him, they deserved some explanation. For the first time he spoke to them to thank them for their mercy. Struggling to speak he tried to blurt out some explanation. He talked about the family, the trip to the temple and how it had affected him. He told how he went there to be close to God and what he found instead. The smells, the noise, the hypocrisy and the commercial side of a place that is supposed to be holy. Then he said it had all become too much and he ran away.

Jesus was surprised at himself for exposing so much of his inner thoughts. "I ran away because I want to find the truth." He added this perhaps attempting to justify his actions. The kindly strangers in orange robes tried to calm their young charge. They told him they were on their way to their home in a far off land. They would be happy to stay with him until he was able to travel. He could then decide if he wished to return home or continue his quest. Exhausted Jesus fell back and slept some more.

The monks watched him as he moved restlessly in his sleep. When he awoke on the third day, Jesus was hungry. He was able to accept food and could swallow what was offered. Then they offered him a rice soup flavoured with a fragrant plant. It tasted good and reminded Jesus how long it was since he last ate. At the same time the kindly strangers changed the dressing on his wound again. They applied a dark sticky substance to his leg and covered it with leaves. The small fire over which the food had been cooked also radiated warmth which made him feel better. And the resilience of youth quickly helped him return close to his naturally curious self.

Jesus felt strangely comfortable in their presence of these kind men who called themselves monks. He wanted to know more about who they were and what they did. They explained again they were Buddhist monks returning from Jerusalem. The group of three stayed camped there on the edge of the city. This gave Jesus leg a chance to heal and his inquisitive mind to kick into full speed to ask a lot of questions. Early each morning at dawn, the monks would take their begging bowls and wander into Jerusalem where they asked for food. According to their vows, they they can only beg for food from dawn till noon. They must fast the rest of the day until the next day when the cycle begins again. When they returned they shared this with Jesus. The monks explained the reason for these actions. They told him of their great founder The Buddha, the awakened one, who was born a prince and given the name Siddhartha. The Buddha, they continued, said that in order for followers to feel part of their religion they need to take part by sharing. It is the duty of the monks to allow others to share their own abundance by giving to the holy orders. All of humanity should learn and love to share what they have, including compassion for the unfortunate. Jesus listened carefully to all of this, and despite his innate caution it made a lot of sense to him. He believed these were men of God and yet they were not Jews. It suddenly became obvious to him that one need not be a Jew to be Godly. Were all Buddhists like these two? Jesus was taking his first step toward an opening his mind.

The monks told him they had felt Jesus had been running away from something and that they sensed his mind was in turmoil, totally confused. He had talked much in his delirium and the emotional experience he had been through at the temple, was still bothering him. It had seemed to them he was running away out of frustration and a feeling of impotence. They had discussed among themselves the possibility of offering to take Jesus with them when they resumed their travel home. However because of his age would he not be better to return home. Here is a youth, frustrated not just trying to find and understand his God, but grasp what it was he himself believed while at the same time live within the laws of his own religion. If he came with us, they reasoned, and learned how others found their way he in turn might find his. They shared these thoughts with Jesus, whatever he wished to do they were there to help.

They explained he was welcome to travel with them or they would help him find his way back to his own home. Jesus took a deep breath looked at these two men and said, "I would be very grateful if I could accompany you. May I ask you a question please?" The monks chuckled a bit and said; "we think you are going to ask us many questions before we part company. Please go ahead." Jesus said you told me you went into Jerusalem with your begging bowls."

"Yes that is right" they said. "What is it you wish to know."

Jesus asked. "Whom did you ask for food, surely there are no Buddhists in Jerusalem. Everyone there is a Jew other than the cursed Romans of course."

The Buddhists looked at Jesus with a smile. "No young master we have developed a Buddhist community several years ago and it is growing. Also you must know there are Gentiles there as well" Blushing Jesus took his second step toward an open mind. The young Jew was on his way, to where he had no idea, but he 'would put his faith in these two men who had befriended him. As they travelled along the roadway they told Jesus how this prince, Siddhartha left his father's palace one day and for the first time saw people suffering, dying, and dead. People so poor they had no place to sleep or food to eat. He saw beggars sitting at the side of the road crying out for something to eat. Living inside the palace grounds he never had an opportunity to see anything other than a life of plenty. He had no knowledge of this side of life. The king his, father, had kept the knowledge of all types of suffering from him. The prince's heart was torn with compassion and pity. He went back home pondering all of this. He thought of his future and then thought of those with no future. His destiny was to be a King someday. His life had been planned for him from before his birth. "Is this what I really want for myself." He knew the answer was 'No.' Something inside of him was telling him there was more he could do and more he could learn. He quietly slipped away from his wife and child, from all the luxury of his home and become an ascetic.

The story continued. The first few years proved to be very difficult. Initially the prince followed a path of renunciation and severe fasting. This left him with little strength. He was unable to even meditate properly. Then he adopted a mode of discipline, more of a middle path, which is more like we monks follow today avoiding the extremes of self-denial and self- indulgence. Years passed, with him living and travelling with other monks or sometimes alone, but always trying to find a way to avoid the suffering in this world. Finally one day he found himself sitting under a large tree with his eyes closed. He slowly began to meditate and allowed himself to be guided. Later he just sort of "woke up" knowing the cause of suffering and now believing the constant suffering of this world could come to a final cessation.

Jesus looked at these to holy men, really seeing them as holy for the first time. He felt their sincerity and humbleness. In his mind he compared them to Caiaphas. They were not Jews but he knew God wrapped them in His love no matter what their religion. Finally speaking in a whisper because he was chocked with emotion, he asked, "did Buddha accomplish what he set out to do?" "To answer your question briefly, yes he did and then travelled a large area preaching and gathering disciples with him as he went.

These he taught to also preach the word.

CHAPTER EIGHT

The trail was dusty and the day hot. Jesus was totally unaware of what was around him, he was deep in thought. He continued to mull over his present situation. Had he done the right thing? He had decided to leave home to learn. It was almost like a decision he didn't have to make. He felt compelled to leave and see:k: drawn to the unknown like a moth to a flame. James instructions in religious matters did not fulfil his desire for knowledge. Even the local rabbi seemed to fall short of his expectations. Looking back now Jesus asked himself. "Who am I to question those who teach?" Every night and many times during the day and night, he would quietly pray to God asking for guidance. In his heart and mind and even physically he knew the Lord was with him guiding him. He even felt it like a physical presence. Finally Jesus decided he had made the correct choice and would stick with it. The strangers were no longer strangers they now had names. In order to make it easier for Jesus to pronounce their names were shortened to Gur and Jit. So the three plodded on moving into the unknown, at least for the youngest member of the group.

Jesus had become a more open-minded person since leaving the temple and realized there was much a world out there and he had much more to learn. At least he hoped so. Was that not what he had embarked on this journey? He was thinking about his former community and their scorn with the Gentiles and the Romans, does God look upon them with scorn too? Is it up to us to judge? When the Pharisees scorn those Jews they considered lower than themselves does God feel likewise. I think not. Jesus upon looking back thought he might have believed he felt compassion for all deep in his heart, this all along, but it was not what he had learned back home. As the three travelled together and Jesus got to know Gur and Jit better, he realized that the the monks were good people who dedicated their lives to helping others. Does God not love them also? He began to turn his thoughts over in his mind. Its it possible that one can be a Jew and recognize the rights and beliefs of others without spurning their teachings and beliefs? He was more open now to the belief that Jews were not better or worse than anyone else. You had to belong to some tribe. He belonged to the Jews. But that didn't mean that he was any more chosen than any other peoples. This actually made him feel stronger and better. He carried his head higher as he walked and breathed deeper: the air clearing his mind. At home these thoughts would never enter his head or heart. He realized now that by leaving home he had opened himself up to experience world. Confidence rose in him like a river overflowing its banks. Jesus knew he had made the correct decision and he was on his way to find answers.

There was one question that was foremost in his mind. Was the God of Israel only a Jewish God or was his God the one and only God of all people? Could it be when God said, you are my chosen people the meaning was not exclusive to Jews? He stumbled and almost fell as they continued along the trail. Tripping on small stones because his mind was had become a common occurrence… The monks would look at him and smile sensing the intensity of this young man. Or Jesus might throw up an arm and suddenly stop in hi track as a new possibility entered his mind. When he did that he would look sheepishly at his companions and grin.

What Jesus knew to be true was that Israel was only small a part of the world. He also knew that there is only one God. Of this there is no doubt. These were the reasons he had chosen this path. New experiences and new beliefs would open the way to total understanding. There might be danger ahead, but Jesus believed God was guiding him. He was likely to encounter much that would challenge he beliefs as a Jew. God wanted him to see life beyond Israel in order to make it all happen.

From his mother he had learned that there were those who worshipped idols. The Torah warned that God is a jealous God and those who worshipped other than him would be punished. But if millions worshipped something other than God did that mean they w0uld all be punished and condemned to an everlasting fate of hell fire and horror? In a short period of time Jesus began to believed that no religion could claim the one and only God exclusively as theirs. His mind must remain open if he was to reach a higher understanding.

The three travellers talked of many things as the days passed and they continued their cross-country trek. They shared much of their individual pasts... Jesus talk about his mother and father and surprisingly of his desire to know God. Jesus' recollections flowed easily, such was the blessing of a young memory. Yet for his part he had a lot he wanted to ask them, however one question in particular seemed too sensitive. Jesus wanted to know about the Buddha and where he fitted into their beliefs. Finally he broached his question. "Is The Buddha the God you worship?" The answer came quickly. "Buddha is not a God. Perhaps in the life he has become a divine person. But we do not recognize just one God as you do. The Buddha had a mission. He wished all people to find wisdom, freedom, peace and most of all an end to all suffering. This he called Nirvana. Our Buddha left the world with the four truths so all could reach Nirvana as he did." Jesus sat staring into the fire, "I need time to digest all of this," he told them with a little smile on his face, he was ready to retire for the night.

Several days passed before that conversation came up again. Jesus enjoyed the daily travel, new vistas, green fields, or yellow fields of ripening grains. Red poppies bloomed in abundance along the well-travelled paths and along side creek beds. Stops here and there with people the monks knew ; small visits with followers who live in little communities along the way. Their modest houses made of red clay offered respite and shade from the midday sun. Jesus was impressed with the serenity and joy their followers who expressed their gratitude with offerings of good no matter how humble. It was given unselfishly; some of them wanting to touch their robes.

It was not surprising then that Jesus had many more questions, but he not wishing to abuse the hospitality of his hosts, thus he held them back until finally he could not restrain himself and he was fit to bursting with curiosity. He remembered his brother James telling him to stop talking and just listen for a change. Here in the middle of this strange land Jesus wanted only to listen. The Buddhist monks were very patient and very compassionate and had no trouble seeing what their fellow traveller wanted. "We think you have a lot of questions and we will attempt to answer all of them. One of the most important things we do, is to explain our way of life. We believe by living a good life while here on the earth it will not be necessary to keep coming back again and again. As a Buddhist our task is to live a life according to the laws of our religion and doing this will hopefully put a stop to the endless cycle of being born again and again, and subject to all kinds of hardships, trouble and misery." Is this not what we attempt to do also, Jesus mused to himself?.

The monks had no trouble seeing that Jesus was not understanding what they were telling him, it showed all over his face. "Do you have a question? If so please ask."

The young student finally said. "Coming back, I do not understand what you mean by coming back." Jesus remembered what it was the Buddha was trying to accomplish. They had told him. A way to help all people to refrain from "coming back to earth again and again." They called it Nirvana. "When our soul leaves the body and we do realize we did not accomplish what we had wished for while here on earth, we are unhappy with ourselves. Our soul has goes back to where we came from. There we review our time on earth and we must come back here in a new body to try again to finish what was left undone from before, or make over what we did wrong last time. Think about this for a bit but see yourself as that soul and ask, did you, Jesus, come back this time with the desire to learn and teach?"

Jesus was shocked. "I did not know I had come back. This suggestion caught the young Jew by surprise. He was left without words. Now 'coming back' was not something about some one else, but it was he who might have come back. Coming back from where? Had he 'Jesus' come back, but back from where? Suddenly the thought had a new meaning. Had he Jesus the son of Mary and Joseph of from the little community of Nazareth been here on earth before in another body? Another person, with another name? He definitely needed time to cope with that question. The monk reached out and touched Jesus arm and said. "You have so much you want to learn, kindly remember that full knowledge takes a long time and will not come in one day. Jesus thought of little else for the next week.

As it happened the three travellers arrived at a village larger than any they had visited before. Here Jesus saw people who covered not just their heads but their faces as well. He learned they were a group called Jains. Jesus asked about them. "You have enough to think about now and you can learn more about them later" he was told.

It was inevitable Jesus would reopen the subject of souls coming back, Jesus often thought about his religious training back in Nazareth. Because he and Thomas were outcasts in their community, he was excluded from studying and training with a Rabbi. It was was not allowed. There was so much he did not know about his own belief. True his mother and brother James had tried to teach them, but here again his impatience had likely deprived him of learning as much as he might. Do my people believe we come back again and again? I do not think so; we ever discussed that at home.

Jesus knew that when one died they would go to heaven to be with God the father, providing they had lived according to the law. Could there be more? It seemed to him that there was much more; perhaps he was just scratching the surface.

So the day came when all three thought it was time to discuss these subjects that had been left hanging. "I have never been taught about souls." Jesus started. "This is something new to me. I believe when one dies they go to heaven and be with God. I know I have a soul, most people do, but that is as far as it goes. How many people stop and think about their soul? If it is true, then we are our soul and not just a human body. When the human mind lives a life that is not in accordance with what we wanted to live here on earth, is it the soul who is punished. Are we that soul? There is so much I have taken for granted without seeing the whole picture. I also have believed since I was a child we Jews are a chosen people and God will look after us. Now I wonder if chosen means what I had thought it to mean. If we are chosen, what are we chosen for or to do. I find it hard to disbelieve my teaching and yet I cannot disbelieve what is in front of my eyes."

The one monk Who went by the name Gur, short for Gurjeet, offered a response to Jesus' queries. Gur's skin was so smooth and Jesus had begun to think of him as the monk with the shiny face. It was he who spoke first. "Yes we are familiar with the Jewish belief in a God of Israel. This is something you must work out for yourself. We respect what you believe and it is possible that without contradicting your previous thoughts you may find there is another way of understanding. As you travel this road you will see many other ways of seeing the same subject. Once three men were arguing about God. The first one said. 'He is the sun see how it makes the plants grow; God is the Sun.' Another who watched a gentle rain give his fields water says, 'God is in the rain see how he gives drink to my plants.' While a third who is tired and needs rest curls up on a large rock warmed by the sun said. 'You are both wrong, God is the wind the that wind blows the rain our way and cools the heat of the sun. Only a God could do that.' "You see my young friend there are many ways to solve the same puzzle. This is probably something you must work out for yourself."

Jesus pondered for awhile thinking. So the Buddha looked for a way to stop the continuation of life after life. Must one be born again only to die and be reborn in an attempt to undo what was done or what was not done in the past life? Is this what the Buddha dedicated his life to do." God would have us live a life of love, charity, compassion, forgiveness, and trust and in doing that one would find a life eternal after this life. Was this what the Buddha was teaching. However he held his thought to himself.

The monks continued. "The Buddha taught us life is impermanent, we call it no self." The second monk whose name was Efors added: "I bring this up to help you understand why we do not think this doctrine of suffering as pessimistic. It is realistic to accept that the human personality and in fact all reality are forever changing. Ask yourself are you the same person today as you were ten years ago or will be ten years from now? If you look at it this way the cause of suffering is not the constant change in itself, but the human desire to hang on to material things, these material things are how we see ourselves, they are what we are. In traditional Buddhism "no self means that there is no permanent identity to continue from one moment to the next. Here is an example: you might look at that stream flowing by and think this is the same stream as it was a moment ago, but it is not. The water you looked at a moment ago is gone and more has taken its place only to also go by. When you look at a candle and the flame you look at seems, constant, but it isn't. It is continuously being replaced by burning. Our selves are like that. You change every minute. If everything changes it is possible for everything to become new. By accepting the doctrine of suffering it is possible to approach even the most difficult situations in life with a sense of lightness and freedom. If a person realizes that there is no permanent self, there is no longer any reason to be attached to all the things that bring someone back in the cycle of death and rebirth. Accepting this realization is enough to start unravelling the chain of causes that bind people to samsara and get them moving toward nirvana. "We respect your beliefs and do not wish to change them. Our philosophy is available to all, but we are a peaceful people and will only go where we are wanted."

"I too am peaceful. Jesus said. I believe in love your neighbour, it is God's way. Some have waged wars to force others to their way of thinking. They have killed those who would not change their beliefs. This is not how I think and would not be part of a religion that forces its beliefs on others. God gave all of us the right of free will. "But wait I do have one more question," Jesus asked and then laughed as he continued, "Should I say another question, please. I often see you walking with your hands in prayer and chanting. Please tell me about that." "We are saying a mantra, it is a prayer, a form of meditation. The words are not as important as the feeling. We become those words, as we are saying them we are living them; we are one with all of eternity. Another way of saying this is, the power of the phrase resides in the syllables themselves rather than in their meaning." Jesus was clearly puzzled.

"Listen to the sound of that water," the monk said as he pointed to the roaring stream beside them. "Allow all other thoughts to leave your mind so your soul can move closer to God, you believe in one God, let this be the path to your God, let the sound of the water be your mantra. As you listen to the water allow all other thoughts leave your human mind and feel God within you."

CHAPTER NINE

The trio of travellers often left the beaten path to reach small Buddhist communities where the monks would hold ceremonies with locals. During these gatherings Jesus was allowed to sit back to watch and hear the message the monks had for their followers. They would set up a small campsite and bring out special holy objects. Occasionally they would build a mound and place a small artifact inside. This will some day become a shrine or a temple to honour The Buddha. The monks would administer to and heal the sick and honour the dead. With much goodwill and fond farewells they moved on. One such side trip, Gur, the monk with the shiny face, said "the Buddha left us with many little thoughts as well as his main messages. One of these I especially like: he said words have their place, but a teaching also can be conveyed through gestures, a smile, a tilt of the head, or even through silence. Buddhism is a teaching about the way to live a serene and contemplative life. One may teach as much by example as by words."

Jesus believed his mission in life was to teach the way of God and he listened intently to everything these men taught him, in hope that these words would broaden his understanding of God's will. Perhaps in a few ways their beliefs were different, but their intent was the same. Love each other and give charity wherever you can. Wherever he went people, saw things differently, but we examined closely the religion of others seemed not as different after all. Yes Jesus was growing not just physically, but more importantly spiritually. He was beginning to see the whole picture. A very apt description.

Strangely enough the Buddhists, even though their beliefs were not the same, never felt threatened by Jesus' own dogma. Nor did they ever attempt to convert him to Buddhism, They allowed him to blend his fundamental understanding with what he was learning and take or reject it as he saw fit. Jesus no longer felt guilt when he learned someone else' point of view, but now understood there was some truth behind it. It was remarkable how these monks had become role models, and they weren't even Jews.

Later they found a place to stop and rest. There was a small stream running through a grove of trees providing delightful shade. It was very hot this day as was most days were. They were tired and need of cool water to rinse of the dust of the trail, as well as a cool drink. This was indeed a good place to camp.

While quenching their thirst at the stream, they heard the sound of voices, little bells, mixed with the sound of hooves and creaking harness. Looking up they saw a caravan approaching from the direction they had just come. It turned out to be a silk caravan heading back to India with goods from the middle east. The men were a mixture of Indians and Arabs. They drove camels and donkeys all laden with goods for markets up the road. Jesus arose from the ground for a closer look. He was still an inquisitive boy and fascinated with all he saw and eager to smell, see, and touch. Despite the heat and dust they brought a feeling of good cheer. A strong young man perhaps eight years older than Jesus stopped and addressed them in Aramaic. "Shelama, my friends may we camp alongside of you?" He was a big man with fierce eyes topped by heavy black eyebrows adding to his fierce look. His dress was white to reflect the hot sun, much as Jesus was clothed. Efors stood up and walked over to greet him. He told them we too are travellers and would welcome their company." Jesus was impressed with the size of the group and while he could not know it at the time he would come to be a close friend of this man and travel with him for years as far away as China. He quickly rid himself of the selfish feeling he immediately had of losing the intimacy of their little group. His first thought was of losing his opportunity to continue to his learning experience. Raj read the look of disappointment on the face of this young Jew and instinctively knew what he was thinking. The wise old man silently whispered. "We will not lose our time together, but in the company of these people we will be much safer on the road ahead."

The new group scattered among the fig trees, helping themselves to the fruit. Jesus observing the unattended orchard thought about his brother Jude who would have kept them pruned and easier to harvest. Thoughts of home often overtook him and a deep feeling of emptiness overtook him. He so desperately wanted to be with his family, but he knew there were many more months perhaps years ahead until he understood what it was he was being guided to learn. It turned out this addition to their little group was going to take him closer to the truth he was seeking. Years later when reflecting on how his life had been guided he would go back to this moment and wonder in awe at the invisible hand that had always been there. When Jesus encountered these mixed feelings he allowed himself to enter that part of his mind that kept him on track. Helping him to push away those lonesome feelings and see the positive. After that he never questioned his decisions looking forward to what was coming next. The monk thanked the leader for speaking Aramaic, He said their young friend was Jewish and could not speak Arabic. "I saw he was a Jew immediately and expected that to be the language of the day." He grinned as he said this and added, "my name is Ishmael, what will I call you my friend?" "I am Gur, my fellow Buddhist here is Efors and the young man is called Jesus. As a traveller I am sure you know Aramaic, not Hebrew is the language most commonly used by the Jews of Galilee, Judea, and Syria. Occasionally Hebrew is be spoken at home usually on a feast day. We speak Aramaic to Jesus as it is the most comfortable language for him." Ishmael nodded and said, "We were in Jerusalem last year and always spoke Aramaic."

That night Jesus walked among the fig trees and prayed to God asking for help to understand the beliefs of others. I am here to learn and sometimes what I learn challenges what I have been taught to believe. Please help me to keep my mind open. Not far away another figure was on his knees also praying. Ishmael was asking the same God in his own way to keep everyone safe in this dangerous part of the world.

Jesus and the monks travelled with the caravan for many months. After the monks departed Jesus travelled to far away

China where he met Buddhists whose beliefs were somewhat different than those of his friends. Jesus wondered why people who believed in the same Buddha could see that leader through different eyes. He thought that is the same with most people who worshipped |God, they argued over the little things when loving God and each other was all that mattered. He would eventually ponder this subject much more in his travels when he encountered religions whose Gods might be earthly objects or even the Sun and Moon. Mankind was gifted with a brain and the freedom of choice; good or bad. How many time had people allowed the love they have for God become hate when encountering other convictions? How many innocents died because of those convictions.

As they travelled Jesus learned the way of the trader, the buying and selling. When they stopped in a town and sold some goods the buyers would argue the price attempting to buy it as cheaply as possible. He was astounded the Arabs would raise the price with some merchants knowing they would need to reduce it. Alternatively when buying Ishmael and his men would argue for hours, even leaving and then coming back in order to buy for as little as possible. For Jesus who had been raised in a barter system secretly believed money was evil, all of this was indeed an education. He had always been aware of the power of greed, but he grudgingly admitted while buying and selling was an important part of living all over, he never for the entirety of his life was comfortable with currency because of the greed that grew from it. As his twin brother I can attest that Jesus could be as obstinate as any person I had ever known. It was both his strength and his downfall. Some said he was mad, many saw him as a God, but he was neither, he loved everybody, and only wanted all to love, share, and see God as a way of life.

One day before the monks departed they told Jesus this story.

"There was a man called Anathapindika who was a danapati or donor who purchased a property for the pleasure and use of the Buddha and his community of monks. He was a layperson just as those the monks had visited and received similar generosity this morning. While generosity is not one of the five moral precepts it is a virtue. Among the other virtues it allows the monks to live a monastic life."

"The lay people have these five precepts: no killing, no stealing, no lying, no abuse of sex, and no drinking of intoxicants. We monks have those and more: We cannot eat after noon, cannot sleep on soft beds, and cannot handle gold and silver. We engage in mental concentration, (Samadhi) this is to focus and clarify the mind and we do prana, which is the understanding of no self. By following these principals we prepare our return in rebirth. The path to Nirvana is divided in eight categories, right understanding, right thought, right speech, right action, right livelihood, right effort, right mindfulness, and right concentration." Jesus was impressed and it showed. Efors laughed and said it seems like much but we reduce these to three, moral conduct, mental concentration, and wisdom. Saying goodbye to these two friends was difficult. The had travelled for more than a year together. Stopping so many places, leaving the beaten path to travel to small villages in order for the monks to meet Buddhist communities, had in itself been an education. Jesus was filled with wonder at the tranquillity and peace these good men brought with them wherever they went. All three wept as they parted.

So it was that a new life opened up for Jesus as he became a member of a trading caravan. A new friendship was born, a new chapter in the life of a young student of the world. Jesus would spend many years with these new friends. They travelled a long way passing through Syria and parts of Persia heading for India. During these trips they would go to out of the way places to buy local products for sale elsewhere. Ishmael and Jesus would have long discussions about what Ishmael called the similarities between the beliefs of a Jew and those of many Arabs. Jesus could not help but see a few similarities between Buddhism and his own Jewish convictions.

Chapter Ten

One day as Jesus and Ishmael were walking side-by-side Jesus asked him about the religion of the Arabs. Ishmael said, "we believe in the same God you do. I am sure you know the story of Abraham and Sarah. Sarah was still childless and Abraham had reached the age of eighty-six. This was a bitter disappointment to him as he wanted a son very much." Jesus knew this story well, but remained silent. Sarah suggested Abraham take her handmaiden Hagar as a surrogate. Abraham prayed to God to guide him in his decision. Believing God would approve Abraham took Hagar and she became pregnant. Hagar delighted in that little one inside her and continually talked about her pregnancy. This disturbed Sarah greatly and had a hard time keeping her jealousy under control even though according to custom the baby would belong to Sarah. The resentment continued until poor Hagar fled the house."

Ishmael continued: "Hagar ran into the wilderness and sat contemplating her fate when an angel appeared. Hagar was told she would have a son and she should call him Ishmael. This will be no ordinary boy, he will be wild and constantly in turmoil with others, never the less he will become a great leader whose descendents would be numerous."

Ishmael stopped and looked at Jesus out of the corner of his eye watching to see how his story was being absorbed. Obviously Jesus was behaving in the appropriate manner so the big man carried on. "Hagar liked what she heard and went back to Abraham's house where she delivered a boy which she called Ishmael." Ishmael stopped again and looking at Jesus with a small grin pointed out he had been named after this child.

"Abraham was eighty- six years old when the boy was born and very proud of this son of his. When young Ishmael was thirteen and according to God's wishes Abraham called all his people around him performed the circumcision ceremony. This son of Abraham's was all his father could have hoped for and they were very close. Then God told Abraham, Sarah will become pregnant and give him another son. Abraham was one hundred years old and Sarah ninety when this miracle happened. Needless to say Abraham was jubilant and celebrated with a feast inviting everyone he knew. He went into the wilderness and made an offering by sacrificing a goat. Abraham spoke to the Lord who promised him his two sons would become great leaders faithful to the Lord God. This child was to be called Isaac."

Jesus had a manner everyone who knew him recognized and this did not escape the eye of Ishmael who noticed Jesus pursing his lips as though he were holding back a question yet not wishing to interrupt. "Go ahead and ask it Jesus. I know you have something on your mind." The Ahab said. Finally Jesus spoke:

"You are right my friend there is a great similarity in your beliefs and mine. You do not call yourself a Jew and yet you look like a Jew and have many customs of a Jew," Ishmael gave a great bellowing laugh. "Many of my people would kill you for saying we are like Jews, but I will receive it as a compliment." So saying he stepped forward and gave the younger and smaller man a huge hug.

Wound up now and even though speaking at this length was very uncustomary, he carried on. When the child was born Abraham called his first son to him and told him he was in charge of teaching his little brother. Isaac grew up following every footstep of his older brother whom he idolized. This rough outdoor young man had a quick temper and was short on patience which meant the youngest would and could receive a quick slap if he did not follow instruction. To all this Abraham heartily approved, but not Sarah. She resented this older boy whom she saw as half animal as well as his mother who she called slave woman. "Abraham send them both away," she would often call out to her husband. This Abraham was loath to do. This was a fine young man and a future great leader also Abraham loved this, his first born, dearly.

One day God called out to Abraham and said I wish you to sacrifice your eldest son, Ishmael. The stricken father could barely control his feelings. He so dearly loved this son and the thought of sacrificing him dismayed him greatly. However Abraham loved his God and respected his every wish so with reluctance he took Ishmael up to the hills and prepared the sacrifice. At the last moment God called out and said Abraham sacrifice a goat, save

Ishmael who will one day serve me as you do. This tells us God saw young Ishmael as a future leader and a great prophet. There are a great number of tribes. They worship several Gods, but we follow the descendents of Abraham and his son Ishmael."

Jesus had been tempted to intervene at one point. It was Isaac who was nearly sacrificed, as this is what all Jews were taught, but very unusual for him, Jesus held his tongue. Neither man could possible know it, but another great prophet would arrive in about six hundred years and unite all the tribes.

Ishmael's voice was giving out. He paused long enough to drink some water from his goatskin to relieve his voice. Offering a drink to Jesus who declined he continued. "I spend too much time walking alongside my camels not talking as much as I am doing now." After a few deep breaths he resumed the story. "Sarah would not relent in her determination to rid her home of Hagar and her son. Abraham finally relented and planned the best way to provide for mother and son in the open space of the wilderness. Before making any decision he asked the Lord to bless his two sons. When the Lord blessed Isaac Abraham asked for a blessing for Ishmael also and the Lord said I have heard thee. I will make him fruitful he shall multiply and have twelve princes and become a great nation. They will live in the east of their brothers the descendents of Isaac. As I have already told you Ishmael will be known as the wild man. He will have many men against him but will triumph."

"Thus it was Abraham finally asked the mother and son to leave, giving them as much food and water as they could carry. He supplied them with two donkeys and a pair of goats. They headed out into the Paran desert where they wandered for days soon losing their way. One day finding a cool clear stream with shady trees all around they stopped and set up camp.

Here tired, discouraged and not a little afraid, Hagar sat with her son and wept. She felt so alone and so lost. Her son hearing his mother's desolation wept too. It was then an angel appeared and admonished her, "why do you cry Hagar did I not lead you to water? God hears you and promises to make Ishmael a great nation. Make your home here and you will be joined by others and become a strong tribe."

"As he grew Ishmael became a great archer and used this skill to fight off other tribes who would seek to take their land. He married and had twelve male children and a daughter who grew up to marry Esau. My personal lineage extends back to a son of Ishmael son of Hagar and Abraham. Our family is known throughout this land, it is this knowledge that keeps us safe as we travel the trading routes.

Jesus asked Ishmael if this story is exactly the way it had been told from generation to generation. Ishmael drew himself up to his full height and fixed Jesus with a stern look, "Exactly word for word. This is the only way we will know who we are and where we came from." The tight little smile he bestowed on Jesus left little doubt his question had been answered honestly.

As the weeks and years passed Jesus hair grew long as did his beard. He developed from a boy to a man. His voice became the voice of the teacher he was to become. Travelling through many countries, visiting many races with their own customs and beliefs broadened his outlook. There were so many people he met too poor to feed themselves while they slaved to make others rich, his resolve to champion the underdog and speak out against greed became stronger.

Travelling to China on one trip, Ishmael suggested they leave the caravan for a short side trip. You have spent time with the Buddhists, but here is more of the same, but at the same time different. I know it all began in India, but when you meet these people you may think this is where it all began. Ishmael and Jesus took a long trail up a mountain and met a person such as he had never seen before. The man looked as though he were one-hundred and fifty years old. (As it turned out he was.) His face was weather beaten with a mass of lines that covered ever part. He was so thin it seemed he never ate food. His eyes were sunken far back in his head, seemed to be looking at Jesus with an intensity that he could feel. He spoke in a language Jesus did not understand, but apparently Ishmael did. After a brief exchange of words the old man spoke to Jesus in his own language.

Here in this very high part of the mountain they saw before them what appeared to be a temple, but who would attend this far away. The answer was quick in coming. This was a training school for young monks. Who lived here until they were fully trained and then sent out to carry their message through out the land. For three days they met and lived with some of the oldest monks Jesus had ever known. This was Tibet a land that seemed to be the sky. Ishmael and Jesus learned many of these people were over one-hundred years old… Their diet consisted of, among other foods, yak milk and a berry that is peculiar to the region. They maintained these berries contributed much to their long life. Also walking up to a place of worship further on kept them nimble and strong.

While they stopped for a drink of tea and some food, Jesus told them of the first two monks he had met and how much he had learned from them. He explained how they had saved his life. They stayed a few days sleeping in very cold huts, covered by Yak robes, but the air was so clean and pure both Jesus and Ishmael felt invigorated and totally alive. When they said their goodbyes and were on their way back to the caravan, Ishmael asked Jesus for his thoughts or impressions. Jesus said, "Since I have been with you I have witnessed many ways to worship a God and what some believed was their God, but the Buddhists are unique, they do not have armies or weapons of war. They do not invade small counties and hold them hostage. They help the poor and homeless. They are good people. I could not be a Buddhist because I worship one God while they believe there are more than one, with not one who is over all the rest. At least that is my interpretation of what I have learned. Yet I admire them and believe God smiles upon them. Buddhists love and to love others, help others is to pray to the one and only God.

Chapter Eleven

Finally they crossed into what is now India. For some reason Jesus felt a sense of excitement, anticipation, perhaps. He was not wrong. Unknown to Jesus Ishmael had made plans for Jesus that would help with the younger man's quest for knowledge. He had done this without Jesus knowing and was embarrassed lest his friend think he was trying to get rid of him. Ishmael knew this would be an exceptional opportunity and taken a chance it would work out alright. It was time to tell him. Accordingly one day as they were walking along side by side he decided this was the time. He had been looking at Jesus getting up the nerve to break the announcement. Jesus had noticed Ishmael's distraction, but decided to say nothing. When the trader was ready, whatever he had on his mind would erupt. That was his way.

Looking around him Jesus had been aware the countryside seemed greener, the vegetation richer, Jesus mentioned this to his companion, commenting on the scenery, but his friend thinking about something else seemed not to hear. Then Ishmael cleared his throat and cleared it again. Finally whatever he was going to say, now was the time. He pulled his friend aside, reached out and took his arm. Jesus could not help a little smile. This was so unlike this bear like man. Then the words gushed out. "Jesus I have made arrangements for you to spend some time with an ancient scholar, I use the word ancient correctly because he is old, very old, but his knowledge goes back a very long way. This land we are entering is itself ancient, some think this is where the very first human was born. I don't know about that but this teacher I am bringing you to has studied all the religion's the country has endured for centuries back. I asked my brother to make the necessary arrangements when he was here the last time."

"I hope you do not mind my friend." He seemed embarrassed. He squeezed Jesus arm and looked at him with concern. "I know I did all of this without consulting you, but I honestly believe you will learn more studying here with this man than you will travelling all over the world with me. I want you to know I am not trying to be rid of you, I love you like a brother, but you have a mission, you said so yourself and this could be the best thing I could do for a brother."

Before hearing any details Jesus knew whatever Ishmael had done was meant to be. It was part of the guidance that had brought him this far. Here was a continuation of the guidance that had been part of his life since he left Jerusalem. It was an answer to the prayer he had made back at the temple.

Ishmael continued, "Jesus I hope you know you are welcome to travel with us for as long as you wish, but I also know of your desire to learn. Under the tutelage of this man you will acquire much of the information you seek. Since we met you have seen many lands and many cultures, but here in this land there is a different heart beat. The pulse of this land is more vibrant. It is as I said mankind might have originated here. You will learn so much and you will love this teacher.

This was the reason for the feeling of something new and exciting just ahead that he had had for days. The sense of anticipation and excitement grabbed him with both hands, it seemed. Oh no doubt the hand of God was at work here. Many years later when Jesus and I were reunited he told me he was constantly amazed at the way his life seemed to be organized without his participation. Back then it was that feeling of spiritual guidance that kept his trust positive. Even when he had no idea what was ahead.

They were entering what is now Pakistan. While Jesus had no idea where he was or where the caravan was going it soon would change direction again and head south into what is now India. The country as it was then was ruled by the Indo Greeks under King Strato. The journey would travel many more weeks stopping now and then to conduct normal business until it reached the town of Ujjeni. Here Ishmael said, "This is the end of the trail for you my friend." Jesus was thrilled and excited he could not wait to meet his new teacher. He was so very grateful to Ishmael, but the bond between the two had grown so strong the parting was going to be difficult. Ishmael was the first close friend Jesus had ever had outside of his family, he was torn between the exciting future and the difficult separation.

All of the rest of the animals and crew stopped for a rest and food while Ishmael took Jesus down a roadway where they could see an old stone building up ahead. It looked to be as old as the very old man who stood at the doorway. He appeared to have seen them as they rounded a corner. His face was lined with many wrinkles, long white hair hung to his shoulders matched by an equally long white beard, below shaggy white eyebrows where a banana shaped nose protruded from this thatch. He was small and thin however his voice when he spoke was strong and surprisingly deep for such a diminutive person. As he stepped forward to greet them Jesus noticed a he shuffled giving him a sliding sort of step. Later he was to discover there was nothing wrong with his legs or feet only his sandals were much too large and constantly falling off his feet. Ishmael introduced him as Vishnu. Who asked them in for a cup of tea. Nothing ever rushed this man as Jesus was to learn later. He graciously asked them to take seats on cushions spread about the floor. When the tea was served Ishmael commented on the flavour. Being a trader who brought teas to this area from afar he praised the quality and flavour of this tea. "It is excellent." Ishmael said as he sipped and asked where is it grown? "Ishmael was surprised to learn it was grown right near the town they were in. An uncomfortable grunt was Ishmael s only response. The Arab imported teas from afar, and was surprised at the quality. A lull in the conversation gave Ishmael an opportunity to arise and embraced Jesus to give a quick almost gruff good bye. Jesus thanked his friend profusely telling him how sad he was to say see him go. Emotional farewells were not Ishmael's strong point. He thanked Vishnu asking him to look after this special friend and was about to take a quick leave when Vishnu touched his arm and told him, "before you leave I want to tell you I am happy to have this new student and do have accommodation for him as you requested. This will be my only student, once more just as you requested." Sensing Ishmael's desire to leave he quickly added. "I hope Jesus will have a long and profitable stay here." With that the big man took a hasty departure, but not before both Vishnu and Jesus noted tears in his eyes.

Vishnu now took both of the hands of Jesus and smiled at him, hoping to comfort what he perceived as a nervous you man. He told him they would travel together over much of the countryside. This will be your class room. While this conversation was in Aramaic Vishnu asked Jesus if could speak Sanskrit. Hearing no, the old man said he would not only teach him to speak the language, but also to read and write it. Jesus asked if it would be possible to learn to read and write Aramaic as well. I shall be happy to do that as well, was his answer.

As Jesus looked at this man who who was to be his teacher he noticed the intense blue of his eyes and how they seemed to be ringed with humour. The old man had a happy look. As he got to know this him better he found Vishnu enjoyed every moment of every day. He disliked no one and found love in everything and everybody. Vishnu was overflowing with compassion and good will. The old man caught Jesus looking him and with a smile on his face said, "are you scrutinizing me to see if I am real, or do you see me as an oddity." Jesus was immediately embarrassed "Master please forgive me, you just look to be so happy and pleased with life I could not help but admire that about you."

"I am happy," was the reply, "I suppose it is because I am content, I have food to eat, a place to live and clothes to cover me. When one is content and not constantly wanting a person lives in love. Now that I have an opportunity to help someone my contentment is greater." Suddenly the loneliness Jesus felt at the departure of his friend was replaced by his own contentment. This caused him to wonder if this ancient man was really human or an angel sent by God to help him. No he mused as the thought continued, there is little doubt he is flesh and blood. Perhaps he is an earth angel, God has many of those scattered around. Jesus had learned from Ishmael his tutor was one hundred and thirty five years old with more years left in his small body. That certainly made him exceptional, even for an earth angel. Grinning Jesus put his arm around Vishnu's shoulder and said, "I do believe it will be easy to learn from you master. It is always easier to remember what one has been taught when the teacher is happy, because when you are happy I will be happy too. "You seem to be such good health for a man of your years, do you have a secret?" "I think I do," Vishnu replied. Each and every day I put twelve drops from a plant called suma in my morning tea and have been doing so since I was a boy. That could be the reason."

Vishnu went on to explain, "as my only student we will be free to travel around and visit people of other faiths such as Hindu, Buddhist, and Jainism. We will see them on their own ground practising what they believe and teach, where they practice what it is they would have you know." Jesus told Vishnu of his time with the Buddhist monks but hastened to add he was sure there was much more to learn. During this conversation they were wandering about the little town talking to many of the locals. It was evident this old man was held in great respect with many asking his advice on a great deal of matters. The student was impressed.

CHAPTER TWELVE

Vishnu began the first day of teaching with an explanation of one of the main religious believes in his country. "We call it our sanatana dharama, this means eternal religion. There have been changes to our beliefs. Please let me explain why. We have been subjected to occupation by other countries who conquered us in order to gain access to our spices, ivory, or you might say our natural resources. Or in many cases just to find land and plenty of water. We have both. They told us they were here to offer protection. Or so they told us. They also brought their religion. There have been many so called protectors. Thus we have worshipped Gods who are human, animals, stones, as well as the sun and the moon. As these conquers come and go we add and subtract gods from our worship. One constant we have is most of us believe, daily, we should be grateful and say thanks. Does it matter if we say thank you to the moon or the sun as long as we understand there is a God who looks after us and we tell him or her thank you. I believe there is only one God so would it not be possible that God is the sun, the, moon, or and idol?"

"Do you not think a divine power has the intelligence to see we are grateful and loving no matter where we find him? How can a loving person hate someone who sees God differently?"

Jesus sat back and thought. Vishnu stopped talking to allow this to sink into his pupil. In the mind of Jesus he was remembering the holy words, *I am a jealous God and you shall have no other Gods but me.* He quietly asked what am I to think God? If I were to see you in a stone or an idol would you be offended? Then the words came into his head clear and strong. 'There is but one God and that God is everywhere in everything including humans. You have God within you and so do all people everywhere. I love all equally and forgive equally no matter what they believe. No one religion is exclusive or excluded. Jesus heard and once more his mind was opening to a broader understanding of belief. Vishnu noted Jesus absence for a moment and knew he was talking to God and God was talking to Jesus. He politely sat quietly.

Vishnu quietly spoke to Jesus. "What did you hear young man? Did not God just speak to you?" Jesus was aghast. "Do you see into my mind master?" The old man looked at Jesus with love in his eyes. "Sometimes when God wants it to be so it is." Jesus continued to stare at Vishnu in disbelief. Perhaps this man is truly an earth angel. "I have sometimes felt you are more angel than human, master." "What does it matter what I am or what you are as long as we accomplish what we wish to accomplish? Therefore what does it matter where we find God as long as we find Him? If in the end we have learned to love and share and forgive, do you not think God will embrace us here on earth and when we return?" The old man laughed and wheezed and then went into a coughing spell until Jesus felt great concern for him. "Are you all right my dear friend?" Jesus leaned forward greatly concerned. Vishnu sat back, his eyes filled with tears from the effort replied. "Yes until I have done what I must do and you are safely on the way back home nothing will befall me."

Vishnu then continued as though nothing had happened saying, "Getting back to what has been part of what we believe, the four holy sites of Buddha are near here and we have accepted many of his teachings and incorporated them into our beliefs. I think keeping our minds open is one of our greatest strengths. Jesus sat and listened carefully. It was going to be necessary to pay attention. This was complicated.

"Many years ago a civilization invaded us settling by the Sindu (Indus) River. They were a well organized people, sanitary, clever, and very artistic. Even though they were invaders they did much for our country building roadways, well-constructed buildings, enclosed sewage drains, and more important to us kept the peace. Along with all of that they introduced their idols which once again we accepted in our easy manner. They lived among us a long time. Until another invader called Aryans moved in and introduced us to Veda which has stayed with us. You will learn more about because it is a large part of what we believe.

We use mantras in four Vedic Samhistas, (collections) which are compiled in sanskrit. They are the Rig-Veda, the Yajur-Veda, the Sama-Veda, and Atharva-Vega. The Rig-Vega are mantras sung and practised from generation to generation as are all the Veda. This is so they will never be forgotten. That began two thousand years ago.

Rig means praise. We believe the hymns of the Rig-Veda and all Vedic hymns were divinely revealed to the rishis, who were considered to be seers or bearers of the Veda, rather than authors. The Vedas are *apaurashaya*, this means uncreated by man. Being from the Gods guarantees their unchanging status. Sometimes we worship elements such as fire and rivers, also there is the god Indra who has lost many followers, but she still gives me much comfort.

Days became months and months soon became a year. Jesus finally had learned to write and read Aramaic as well as Sanskrit. He realized he had changed so much. While he still considered himself a Jew, his acceptance of other beliefs as something recognized by God had become easier to accept. No one who said thank you to whatever their concept of God, loved others, were compassionate, and charitable, these had found the one and only God. Thinking back to his years in Nazareth, he had come a long way.

One day seeing Jesus was restless, Vishnu suggested a change. "There is a large community of Jews who live not far from here, would you like to meet some of your countrymen? The look on Jesus face was his answer. Excited he agreed willingly. Vishnu explained further, "these people fled Roman rule and eventually found their way here. I believe you will find them as excited to meet you as you are to meet them." The two of them set off walking to a different part of the town Jesus had never seen before.

On the way Jesus saw a small gathering of people who seemed excited, obviously enjoying themselves. Seeing this and looking for some excitement himself Jesus wondering what was happening hurried over, leaving his old instructor behind. Arriving there ahead of Vishnu he pushed himself in. The crowd being good natured moved aside for this stranger. Vishnu finally caught up and worriedly shoved in beside him.

They watched as a man walked on live coals in his bare feet, upon reaching the end turned around and walked back and stepped off the coals turned to the crowd. Jesus saw the entertainer had sharpened sticks protruding from his lips and other parts of his body. He then pulled the sticks from his face and strangely enough there was no blood. This type of performance would never be seen back home so Jesus watched fascinated. He could not understand why anyone would wish to hurt themselves. The performer saw Jesus in the crowd and walked over to see him. Vishnu quickly whispered, "He normally speaks in Persian, but you may talk to him in Sanskrit which he also speaks." The young man said, "My name is Arjuna, I see you are one who has lived on this earth before. I believe you are a holy man I can see you are different. Should you questions I would be pleased to answer them? He spoke in Sanskrit without being told to do so. Jesus replied, "How do you bear the pain and also keep from injuring your self?" "My mind controls my body and tells it there is no pain and no blood shall issue forth. My higher mind over rides my human mind. You are here to help the helpless, this I think, is that not so?" Jesus did not reply but would never forget the conversation.

Continuing their walk, they passed through a very poor part of the town. Here Jesus saw huts made from branches, grass, or anything that could be used for shelter. The huts looked endless as they went on row after row as far as he could see. People dressed in rags, bodies skin and bone. Many deformed begging in a language unknown to him. This was the first time he had seen poverty like this. Jesus found he was holding his breath in sorrow for these people. His heart wept for them. Silently he lashed out at the inequity of life. This is not the way God wishes mankind to treat each other. Then he remembered the story of Buddha and his reaction in a similar situation and he understood.

As he stood transfixed looking at this little city of beggars, a small girl approached him, stood at his side and looked up into his eyes. She was so thin, obviously a beggar her clothes hanging in rags. Her legs looked as though she had been whipped. Her hair was matted and dirty She stared at him as though he might not be real. It was then she reached out and touched him. He looked down at her noticing for the first time her face had the same deformity as his sister Ruth. His mind flashed back to his sister and suddenly he was overwhelmed partly because of Ruth, but mostly for this tiny child. Emotion, love and compassion flooded over him. Unconsciously he reached out, took both of her hands and said in the name of God let her be whole as God intended. With that he passed his hand across the child's face and as his hand moved away all who watched saw her features take on a look of pure beauty, the deformity completely gone. While the little girl did not know what change had taken place those standing by most certainly did. Jesus holding his hands together over his mouth looked upward and thanked God.

Vishnu quickly grabbed him by the arm and said we must leave here now or you will be in grave danger. For the first time Jesus saw the reaction in the crowd as they began to move toward him shouting trying to touch him. Teacher and student fled.

They hurried down narrow alley ways and found a busy street filled with shops. Hurrying along as fast as Vishnu's old legs would go Jesus saw many Hebrew symbols and lettering, some of which were in Aramaic. It did not occur ti him he could read until he found himself understanding the signs before him. He stopped and said, "if I did not know better I would think I was in Jerusalem."

Vishnu could not hold back the smile on his face as he said, "we call this little Jerusalem. There are many people here who came from your part of the world and would like to meet you." They stopped in front of a stall where a merchant came out to meet them, obviously a Jew. Jesus was filled with emotion. It had been a long time since leaving home and he longed for his countrymen. The young student could not hold back his tears of joy. It was almost time for the feast of Passover and Jesus had not celebrated any holiday since fleeing Jerusalem, many years ago. He prayed to God for forgiveness every time he was unable to take part in a. Holy day.

As they introduced themselves more Jews came from their shops to join the little crowd. Vishnu made the introductions and explained the presence of his student. These fellow Jews were not about to allow this new country man to leave too soon and asked him to stay until after Passover and beseeched Vishnu to allow Jesus to remain amongst them. The elderly scholar agreed and promised to come back to pick him up.

CHAPTER THIRTEEN

The enjoyable time with his fellow countrymen over and Jesus back once more with his instructor he asked Vishnu a question that had been on his mind since there visit to the man who walked on coals. Master when I was talking to the man who walked on fire he whispered in my ear, "you have been here before and now you are back to help the helpless." Vishnu did not respond, but sat quietly allowing Jesus to carry on. "Was I here before? What does that mean. Vishnu smiled for he knew this subject would come up they had been talking around it for some time. The answer was part of what this young man needed to learn.

"Yes I believe you were here before and now have come back. Remember the Buddha and the task he gave himself? He saw so much suffering and felt most of it was needless. He looked for a way by which all people might live right and not need to come back to try to redeem themselves. A way they could love each other as they love themselves, help the needy, find a way in which all could live correctly and never need come back to this earth only to do it all over again."

Watching Jesus to be sure he was understood, he continued. "We are all two parts and at the same time one. We came to earth as a soul to live in a human body with a human mind. The perfect way is both, human and soul, live as God would have us do. In other words live as one. We would share our wealth; love each other as we love ourselves. From your point of view keep God in our lives. Some of us allow the human ego to take over and shove the soul aside to live a life of greed and selfishness. They forget the poor even using them as slaves in their search for more human possessions. Greed has replaced God and greed has robbed the soul of its original intentions here on earth. The soul has lost control or decided to live as a human and when this happens must come back to live as a human once more.

"Teacher if I was here before does that mean I failed in my last life?"

"Not necessarily, there are some whom God chooses to send back to help those who struggle. Prophets, and healers, teachers and even some who choose to come back maimed and poor. The latter to live among the more fortunate giving them an opportunity to help the unfortunate. To be an example you might say. Some will die as martyrs in order to bring attention to the disorder mankind has created. I believe you might be one of those. A chosen one. Later Jesus sat and thought about what he had just learned and strove to understand how and what he would teach should he be a chosen one.

Did God give Moses the key to living the perfect life when he gave him the ten commandments? Was this a pattern to live life by and in doing that find happiness here on earth; heaven here on earth.

How many really understood their own soul or even know they have one and in doing so lose God?

Where does one find God?

Vishnu said God is where you seek Him.

God lives in all of us. So look within. Live as you planned before you were born.

During a later session Vishnu said "today I will introduce you to another religion of this country. Here are more who believe in reincarnation. This is called Jainism and in a number of ways you will find much of what they believe to your liking. For these people are a peaceful society. They never make war. Jain Dharma is an ancient religion found here in this country as is Hinduism and Buddhism. These people prescribe a path of peace and non-violence toward all living beings. The philosophy and practice depend much on self effort in the progress of the soul on the spiritual ladder to divine consciousness. Any soul which has conquered its own demons and achieved the state of a spiritual advanced being is called jina. This means conqueror or victor. Jains are a very literate group. Their insistence on scholarship goes back a thousand years. Jains regard every living soul as potentially divine. Is this not a message for all humans? We come to this earth from a place of perfection to seek divinity in a human form thus to return having accomplished what we came for. How many humans work at self effort, non-violence, love of neighbour as well as love of God recognizing their soul as who they really are? I wanted you to learn something about the Jain

Dharma even though you may not be able to accept their entire philosophy it seems there is something in all beliefs that leads one toward God."

"Because each Jain is encouraged to rely on their self for spiritual development and cultivate their own personal wisdom and self control that goal is buried deep within. Therefore dedicated to saving their own souls they take on the responsibility of their own salvation. The goal of Jainism is to realize the souls true nature. These are the triple gems of Jainism. This they call moksha. Moksha provides the path for attaining liberation from samsara, the cycle of birth and death. Does that sound familiar? Those who have attained mosha are considered liberated souls which they call siddha."

"Those who remain attached to worldly possessions are called mundane souls.

Dull people whose God is money."

Vishnu stopped for breath and looked at Jesus closely see if he had a better understanding of life after life and why some must be born again.

Jesus did have a much better understanding and was thinking about each persons connection to God and to each other. Looking back at what he now knew about the beliefs of his people, the Buddhists, the Hindus, and now the Jains, he could see God at work in what each believed. God loves all equally and no matter how each one reaches out to God it matters most how we treat each other, for God is in each of us. When we love each other we are in fact worshipping God. God is love. That is where you find him. Without love there is no God.

Praying without sincerity is not praying it is only lip service in which there is no love. To memorize a prayer and say it without thinking it is not a praying. Even a mantra must be said with thought.

"One more thing Jesus, The Jains believe that the Universe and Dharma are eternal, without beginning or end. The Universe undergoes processes of cyclical change. This same Universe consists of living beings and non living beings. All worldly relations of living beings with other living beings and non living beings are based on the accumulation of Karma and its conscious thoughts, speech and actions carried out in its current form.

There is a lot of emphasis on the consequences of not just your physical form,… but on what you think. Thoughts are a form of life. *Thoughts are energy and carry an unspoken message.*

There was much to think about and Jesus knew his own thoughts had changed much since he left home. If God wanted him to take what he had learned and tell it to all who would listen there was much here that would offend the priests and rabbis back home. Jesus liked the non-violence and the path of peace toward all living beings. Striving to climb the ladder to a divine consciousness was what all people should be doing. It was a matter of fundamental knowledge the vast majority would not take on this personal task. Conquering one's own inner demons meant conquering anger, hatred, lack of charity, sexual habits out of control, jealousy, killing and greed. To regard every human as potentially divine would be a huge step toward your own divinity thought Jesus with a bit of a wry smile. He now knew life after life and living with your own soul would be an important part of his teaching. Jesus went for a walk by himself trying to organize his thoughts. It seemed to him it was time to go home and begin his life's work. He knew now what it was he must do.

Forgetful of where he was going and so deep in thought he wandered back to that area where he had healed the little girl. Vishnu had often told him it was unwise to go out alone especially in those parts of Ujjeni where all the very poor lived. Reaching that part of town again he saw a boy sitting on the ground with a crude wooden bowl held out in front of him begging. It seemed obvious someone must have carried him to his place of begging. It was obvious his thin twisted legs would not have permitted him to walk on his own. Jesus did not carry money or even food to offer this child. From deep inside of him he heard the voice of God calling on him to help the boy to stand on his own. "Here is one who will one day work for all of his people." Jesus heard God's voice and was filled with compassion and love for this child. He reached down lifted him to his feet, the child reacted with terror fearing he would be slapped, as so often happened. When the boy saw the look of love and compassion on the face of this stranger his fear changed to wonder and surprise. Jesus held the boy upright, and speaking to God said, "heal him, give him full use of his legs. Make them strong and complete, in the name of all that is good." The boy suddenly became aware of a new strength flowing into his legs. He could feel his feet and then the strength flowed upward to his thighs. As Jesus took his hands away the boy stood on his own for the first time in his life. A look of utter amazement appeared on his face. He first moved his feet, then walked. At first a few tentative steps and then in total joy and wonderment he began to walk around in circles. There were a few on ht street who had seen this miracle. They gathered around him touching, patting and uttering words of praise for this miracle man. Vishnu who had followed, moved to steer Jesus away from a fast forming crowd. Before he left, Jesus patted the young lad on the head while Vishnu spoke to the boy in his own language. Then the two were gone. "May I ask what you said to that boy Master Vishnu?" "Yes" Vishnu replied, I told him to thank God for his miracle and prepare to help his people as he will become one of his countries great leaders." Jesus looking at the teacher and said "how could you know that? For that is what God said to me." Vishnu smiled and looked at Jesus saying "God works his wonders in many mysterious way. It is for us to believe and expect His power when we ourselves are filled with his love."

As they walked along a pathway back home, Jesus took Vishnu by the arm pulling him to a stop and said, "my good friend and teacher, I believe it is time to go back where I came from." Vishnu agreed.

CHAPTER FOURTEEN

The journey back home was long and tiring, Jesus knew it would be so, but it would give him time to collect his thoughts and prepare himself for the life ahead. Before leaving while each was saying a heartfelt goodbye, Vishnu handed Jesus a purse filled with money. "This is from your friends in little Jerusalem, Ishamael, and myself may God protect you and guide you along the way. You are meant to become a great influence on this earth both while you live and after."

As much as Jesus longed to once more be united with his family saying goodbye to this wonderful old man was sad. Now approaching thirty years of age Jesus was a man in every sense of the word. He most certainly had matured in the past fourteen years, yet he still had that impetuous zeal of youth. His desire to fight greed and cruelty never wavered. His heart was always with the unfortunate and always would be. Why can life on earth not be a joy for every person, he would say? Those born into poverty only to die in poverty would always be closest to his heart. He would always work for them. He suspected that wherever you find humanity, there would be both rich and poor. With all of this he could see why God's word needed to be taken far beyond the borders of Israel. He would need many helpers.

As he walked along a hot and dusty road he remembered the Buddhist monks and their words. Both they and the Jains believed in a life without violence. Love and compassion were foremost in their beliefs. Most religion's had similarities yet unfortunately so many saw the differences before the beliefs they shared.

As he travelled he met others who travelled the same path. Jesus found this most enjoyable, they would walk together, often camp together and share what food and water they carried. Later in the companionship that travellers often found they would share their experiences. Telling each about their lives and customs. Jesus had so much he could talk about and noticed how his stories were received with such interest. There was no doubt he was a good speaker and getting better as time passed… some travelling in the opposite direction would bring stories from home. Jesus longed to hear such messages.

It was a long tiring trip, one that took much out of him. He ached to be home knowing there was much to be done. Thoughts of family were uppermost in mind. How would the family greet him when he returned? Would he have changed so much he looked like a stranger? No; he knew in his heart they would still love him and accept him.

At long last he entered Nazareth. His eyes sought familiar buildings and most importantly familiar people. His heart beat faster as he drew closer to home and his excitement grew. Jesus recognized himself as an impatient man and that impatience was growing. He walked faster. Scanning each face looking for a loved one. A person passing called out, "good day Thomas you must be working harder than ever you're losing weight." Jesus giggled at that remark. Then he rounded a corner and saw his mother's house, his heart seemed to leap into his throat. He was actually short of breath and then, he saw her standing by the door looking up the road sheltering her eyes from the sun. He called out "mother." Mary could not believe her eyes even though when she awoke that morning she felt this is the day.

She looked older, but then she was fifteen years older. Her hair was grey and yes there was a stoop in her posture, but this was Mary his mother and now he really choked up. His heart could not beat any faster, but his legs ran faster. Tears filled his eyes. As she saw him she began to run toward him calling "Jesus Jesus I knew you were coming today, knew it, just knew it." Then she was standing close with her arms around him, touching him, kissing him. "Oh how I have missed you, but I knew you were in God's good hands and always safe," she cried. The words flowed out one after the other sometimes not totally coherent but Jesus knew every word she said. He found it hard to talk, never the less this moment was everything he had hoped for. Here was his dear mother in his arms and words were not necessary. He was home. Thank you God.

The family were one again. They gathered together and enjoyed the intimacy of this occasion. Special foods were prepared and served. When Jesus saw Ruth for the first time he looked at her face and remembered the little girl in Ujjeni. In his mind he reached out to God and an unspoken prayer asked for the healing for his sister. (Dear God if it be your will let her face be as she always hoped it would be.) He touched her face with both hands covering it completely. He could feel the change taking place beneath his fingers as he kissed her forehead. Then all in the room expelled could hear the sharp intake of breath from Ruth not knowing what was happening. When Jesus removed his hands from her face even Jesus was amazed it was indeed beautiful. The others gasped in astonishment while Ruth not being able to see what had happened knew in her heart a miracle had occurred and ran from the room to see for herself. The miracle of Jesus return combined with the miracle of Ruth's face set the course for the path he was to follow.

They spent the evening exchanging stories, of course it was Jesus who had the most to relate. James had been quiet not knowing what his younger brother had been doing, but finally became a believer when he saw what had happened with Ruth. He had been taken on at the temple as a teacher and had become a highly respected teacher. Also he was married and a father. Secretly he wondered what the return of Jesus would do to his position with the head priest and leaders? Knowing his brothers passionate temperament combined with his experiences while away his brother was not going to lead a passive life. Thomas was overjoyed to have his brother back. He longed to have him away by himself to hear more about his life since they parted and also his plans. Jude had also married and lived on the property. Ethyl and Jacob had died their rooms filled with a growing family.

Mary sat quietly listening to the excited conversation. As she looked at her twin boys she saw how identical they still were in appearance, yet so far apart in temperament. Thomas quiet, loving, understanding and humble, he must be dearly loved by God. Jesus on the other hand was fiery, positive, and dedicated. He was truly God's man on earth. Where would his goals take him? What were his goals? What danger lay before him? A mother's love for a child caused an involuntary shudder to pass through her. She quickly buried her fears and just looked at him, loving him. This was a time for rejoicing.

Jesus found Thomas's occupation as a boat builder interesting and wished to learn more about his brothers occupation. He asked Thomas to spend a day with him discussing some ideas he had. Somehow the boat building and its location seemed to be part of an abstract idea. Or at least the people involved. If you asked him what it was he was thinking he would tell you he had no idea. True, he didn't.

The next day when Thomas and Jesus were together Jesus told his brother what it was he wanted to do. The brothers sat side by side while Jesus told Thomas all about what he had learned and how he had grown spiritually. He told him of Ishmael and Vishnu and how they contributed so much to his experiences. "Travel to the sea with me Thomas, introduce me to your friends and we will start there. Thomas come work with me help me to do God's work. Together we will change the world. Thomas head was swimming with the excitement of his brother. The Jesus went on to discuss the importance of recruiting others to help spread the message. We cannot do it alone he said. It will be necessary to have disciples and you will be my first. Thomas my dear brother God wishes us to tell everyone of his love and forgiveness. He wants us to speak out against greed and above all help people to understand it is their own souls they are saving. We are all equal in his eyes, not matter how we worship. Our task will be to take this God's message to all the people.

Jesus and Thomas found themselves by the sea. Here Jesus saw first hand what work his brother did and also had a chance to meet others who worked there. Jesus never knew why, but the type of people whom he found here represented the type of individual he would draw on for his followers. Thomas introduced Jesus to his friends who eagerly asked him about other countries and those who lived there. He told them of their beliefs and way of living. How they worshipped God and how they lived. It was not long before a small group gathered together and Jesus went on to tell them how greed was as prevalent there as it was here. How armies would sweep in and take over a country leaving new ways of finding God. But how there was only one God for all people. He told them of their own souls and how it was important to live according to the way God would have us live, and then he told them about life after life. He told them how the Buddha strove to find a way to live to avoid coming back over and over.

Day after day he talked and taught and the crowds grew larger. It was not long before one person telling of his message to others his the fame as a rabbi grew.

Weeks became months and the word of this man who spoke the truth simply and without anger spread throughout the land. He talked of love, charity and God. Occasionally he would heal someone who was suffering. As he met those with inflictions his heart went out to them. He explained why it was necessary to come back to earth only to be born again to find Gods way in human form. He often referred to the Buddha who also despised greed. As God forgives you, so you should forgive each other. Some would ask if he worshipped the Buddha and Jesus answered no, the Buddha is not a God, but a prophet who wanted to ease the suffering of people while on earth.

One time as he was telling the word of God he met two women name Martha and Mary Magdalene. He had noticed them in the crowds before. After finishing for a day he singled them out and spoke to them. They had heard his message before and now Mary wished to became a disciple. Jesus eagerly accepted her so after Thomas she became the second to become one of his followers. Sometimes when the three were alone, perhaps sitting and eating he would talk of his years in India and the caste system he saw there. He then compared it to the same thing he saw in Jerusalem. Caiaphas the high priest who saw differences in their own people singled out the Pharisees who he said lived apart and were hypocrites. Also the Sadducee who would divide the Jews. This prompted Jesus to say when you divide a kingdom you divide the love of one for the other. God means for all people to respect and care for each other even though they live in other countries. Those who would invade other counties for the sake of riches and land only to enslave the population have turned their back on God.

His followers grew once more as Mathew, James, John stepped out from the crowd and asked to become part of the Rabbi's followers. It was not long after that Peter and Andrew came to Jesus and said we have heard what you say and would be part of those who help to spread the word. Thomas had known Peter and

Andrew for some time. They were fishermen and met Thomas who built boats and in this found a commonality in the sea. They had know each other for a long time. It turned out they had been in the first group Jesus had spoken and now after hearing Jesus speak again they knew what they must do.

One day the little group of eight were invited to a large home for dinner where many others were also invited. The food was excellent and the wine was the very best. These were people who used currency to buy all their needs including friendship and favours. Jesus was aware of this and while his views on currency had softened only somewhat during his years away, he still clung to his belief that the disparity between those with much and those with none had only strengthened. His trip home could not have worked as well as it did without money and for this he was grateful. He never could understand why a person could hoard money just for the sake of owning it. Money tends to promote greed he would often say. Those with more than they need should be helping those without.

When he spoke to the gathering, he told them about the very poor he had seen in a far off country and how it was necessary to beg for mere scraps. He referred again to the Buddha who had been a prince and gave it all up when he saw the sick, the poor and the destitute. In the telling he went on to discuss the need of the soul to judge itself when reliving its time on earth. The conversation eventually led to each persons soul in the room and it's relationship with God. Your soul is you. The human body in which you now reside is only temporary. Listen to what I tell you it is not too late to save yourself. His voice deepened and his eyes flashed as he pointed at the group. Love your neighbour and love your enemy, he shouted now. Learn to forgive, be charitable. To many this was so new and as Jesus continued to speak the group gathered their robes closer as though cold, but they moved closer asking questions, wanting to hear more.

To answer their questions Jesus went on to tell how a soul comes from heaven to live in a body when it is born. The soul wishes to guide the human to live a fruitful and helpful life. When the soul becomes so human it sees itself as part of humanity, becomes discontented, wants more, possesses more, eventually takes from others and accumulates money just for the sake of owning it, thus loses its contact with God. When the body becomes dust it must return from whence it came and there in the presence of perfection it must then judge itself. No harsher judge than oneself while in the presence of God can be found.

In the group was an elder from Jerusalem who went back to the the high priest Caiaphas telling him of this so called rabbi that was preaching contrary to the bible. He related what he had heard Jesus say to Caiaphas and the elders who had gathered together to hear the report. They listened in shock and railed out in anger at this blasphemy. Who is this so called rabbi who speaks such words. He must be brought to justice. They had the elder repeat over and over again the message of this man. This was the beginning of the resentment that would put fear in the hearts of the high priest and his elders. The foundation for the charges which were to be laid against Jesus were laid in that room. As if this elder had not said enough he added, "This man said we are all equal in the eyes of God even Gentiles and Romans." The die was cast.

CHAPTER FIFTEEN

"There is no need to feel alone and frightened when God and his mercy are part of our lives," Jesus would say as he stood under a tree talking to a large group. "Live with God in your life and you will never be alone. Remember greed is the way of evil and evil leads to self destruction. If you look at beggars and turn your back, you are living without God. When your day has come to leave this world you must go back and judge yourself. Seek the Kingdom of God now while you are here in this life and live forever in the Kingdom of God." One person in the crowd called out, "Master where is this Kingdom you speak of, how would I find it"? Jesus stopped and seeing the speaker said, "Look around you. Open your eyes the Kingdom of God is here within you." Whenever and wherever he spoke those who heard him became believers and that is what was sealing his doom.

As the crowds became followers in ever increasing numbers this information kept coming back to the high priest Caiaphas who would fly into a rage increasing his determination to rid himself and the world of this man. He would never admit it but along with his anger there was also a deepening fear his position was threatened. "What utter nonsense," he would tell himself, that cannot happen, but the doubt would not leave him.

As Caiaphas pondered his big question, he admitted to himself it would weaken his position if this one man were seen to frighten him. While his mind chewed on the issue a new thought came to him. Why not seek help, someone with power who could take the responsibility of the action he had in mind. One who might benefit by the removal of this man Jesus. No better person than Pilate the commanding officer of the Roman army. Since Herod had died and his weak son had taken his place, Pilates power had grown. As the High Priests thoughts warmed to this idea he knew there were other reasons Pilate might be very agreeable. There were rumours coming back from Rome about a feeling of antisemitism growing back there. Ever the politician, Pilate had disguised a large troop of soldiers as Jews hidden weapons in their robes and infiltrated Jewish protestors who were already inside the Temple. The soldiers created a riot and eliminated many protestors resulting in the death of a number of Jews. The survivors realized it was Roman soldiers who had infiltrated the temple. They were angry, rebellious and calling for justice. Perhaps this had been a mistake on the part of Pilate. It was not long ago that a man named Simon had rebelled and needed to be subdued. Pilate would not want another rebellion. Could this man Jesus be presented as a threat? Perhaps if it was put to him in the right way this could be an opportunity. Pilate could ingratiate himself with Tiberius once again by ridding another Jewish troublemaker. It would be necessary to show him as that. The cunning mind of the high priest seized upon this thought, but knew it would need to be handled skillfully.

There was another matter that was of concern to Caiaphas. A situation of severe importance. The Sanhedrin. This was a council of over seventy members dominated by the Pharisees. Their mandate was to guide both Pilate and Caiaphas on matters of civic and cultic importance. They annoyed the high priest by interfering with matters in the temple, primarily the sale of sacrificial animals to the public for sacrifice. Their single-mindedness to the old laws was almost fanatical. They left no room for Caiaphas to manipulate the Temples management to his benefit. Yes he needed the power and backing of the Roman army. There was little doubt in Caiaphas mind that Pilate would be aware of Jesus and his influence in the community. The soldier missed little.

Dealing with the Sanhedrin was a delicate matter. After all they were the watchdogs of the Jewish law, but to many considered extremists. Caiaphas in particular. Money was not permitted in the Temple itself, according to Pharisees teaching, but in order to buy a sacrifice in the great court, and that is considered part of the Temple, it turned the building into a market place. Caiaphas disagreed. How could the Temple be what it is without the profits generated by merchants. Any fool knows that. To make matters worse this was one of the points the man Jesus preached against. Another reason to get rid of him. Jesus had heard of Pilates deception and massacre of innocent Jews and called upon both Caiaphas and Pilate to be held accountable for this tragedy. When you added up all these points it was clear, Jesus must go.

Jesus did nothing to soften the anger he was building against himself and nothing to slow the plans of the high priest. I had always said the stubborn streak of Jesus would get him into trouble. Jesus had said maybe that is why I am here.

So it must happen. This the most powerful Jew in Israel would take steps to rid himself of two thorns in his side. Caiaphas would move the Sanhedrin away to nearby Mount Olive and out of the Temple with the support of this powerful Roman. The trouble maker Jesus would be arrested by Pilate. Even if that troublesome Roman did not know it he soon would. Caiaphas chuckled at his own cleverness.

A meeting with Pilate was arranged. Both the Sanhedrin and the trouble maker Jesus were to be discussed.

Pilate and Caiaphas were about to become allies. Neither liked the other, but necessity brings many alike people together. Pilate ordered the meeting at his headquarters and this irked Caiaphas not a little he would have loved Pilate to have come to him even though it would be bringing a Roman into the temple.

Jesus had chosen to move his of teaching to Jerusalem and the Temple itself. He knew this to be a dangerous step, but the word of God must be told everywhere. I called upon my brother to heed the growing danger, but he told me if he was to accomplish God's work there was no turning back.

Therefore we all went to the Temple once more. I suggested to Mary Magdalene there could be danger and perhaps she should stay away. She said her place was with Jesus also she was the unofficial leader of the disciples.

On the way up the hill Jesus accosted the merchants and told them to take their business elsewhere. This is the house of the Lord not a place of business. I suppose Jesus knew his outburst was useless, but he felt it was good for the visitors who stood nearby. The merchants sat quietly while he spoke and did not respond they did not need to. They paid no heed for the high priest received a portion of their profits so when they had a problem they complained to the authorities. Jesus condemned the use and needless slaughter of animals which also produced an income to both the high priest and his associates. Once more this radical preacher was a subject of derision by those whose life depended upon commerce. Regardless of the tension that was mounting Jesus stood on the steps and spoke to all who would stop and listen and that was many.

The high priest was fully aware of this man from Nazareth was in the temple but rather than confront him he stayed back and listened here was a chance for Caiaphas to see and hear this man Jesus in action. Standing away from the group but close enough to hear he heard him say "all men are equal in the eyes of God, God dwells in the heart of all people no matter what their beliefs." "When we are born our soul enters the body and lives with us for our entire lives. That soul is us and we are that soul. When you choose the path of greed and are not charitable you ignore the will of God. Money is the tool of the greedy and brings evil into the hearts of those who would see it as their God. You must share with those who have nothing. Love thy neighbour as thyself no matter what his or here race or religion. Forgive your enemies we are all equal in His eyes." These words fell upon the ears of the priests and elders like a blow. Caiaphas standing behind a pillar heard it all. He joined them now and moved to accost Jesus asking him by what authority does he preach in this holy place? Jesus quietly replied, "The Lord himself asked me. "Do you say the Lord God speaks to you." "Yes." Jesus said. He would speak to you also, if you speak sincerely with love in your heart" These words decided his fate. There was no turning back.

Chapter Sixteen

The fateful meeting between the powers took place on a warm day. The smell of the season was in the air and everything considered this should be a productive day. At least that was what Caiaphas was thinking as he looked around at the luxurious surroundings of Pilate. The high priest sniffed as he saw the Captain had put out food and drink. It did not help his mood when two smartly dressed soldiers crossed their spears and refused him entrance until their leader bade them allow the chief priest to enter. Pilate listened to all Caiaphas had to say and looking at this temple official shrugged his shoulders and said, "do as you wish. Caiaphas was not through and not ready to be shrugged off lightly. He asked if Pilate knew of the man Jesus he had been talking about. 'Yes' the captain responded. 'I am aware of this man, I have been hearing people talk and sent some people out to listen… Actually, some of the things the rabbi Jesus said were quite interesting." Those words fell on the high priest's ears like a personal blow. His hatred for the man grew to a hot point. Nothing more could be gained by remaining longer, he declined the food and left.

We disciples knew that tension with the authorities was mounting and could not be discounted. We all begged Jesus to go away for awhile and save himself. Jesus looked at us as we gathered round him and said," "to run away would undo all we have accomplished. We must trust my remaining here is what the Lord God would wish.

Word came back, attributed to Caiaphas himself, "Jesus preached against Jewish law and that is treason. He also said we are all born equal even the Romans and that makes him a criminal."

These comments by the high priest came back to Jesus, he responded by saying, "I was born a Jew and I remain a Jew. I live by Jewish law, but I do not recognize all that this local counsel claims to be law. Some misinterpret the law to work for their own benefit. The God we worship is the same God all worship no matter what they call him. There is but one God. If some find what I say to be wrong let them tell it to the Lord God. If that same God comes to me and tells me I am wrong I will stop my preaching and teaching and I will go away."

On the first day of the feast of unleavened bread we asked Jesus where he wished to eat the Passover. Jesus said we have all been invited to celebrate the Passover with a friend at his house. With those words we set off for this friends home. Later he gathered us all together and said, "we must have some time to plan ahead. Danger is at hand and changes are about to happen. We have discussed what will happen if I am no longer here. You will all continue to preach Gods word as I have done. It is likely I will be arrested and taken away, I do not know how long they will keep me. I want you to remember the word of God must be taken to far away places as well as here. God is with you as He is with me. We have discussed where each of you will go, but whatever place you go to please remember my heart is with you always."

It was that night Pilates soldiers came and took him away to stand before Caiaphas, his priests and elders who sat as a jury to try him. Witnesses were called to testify against him. They were asked if Jesus had said all were equal in the eyes of God, and they answered yes. They testified he said unless you love and share with each other no matter who they may be you deprive the Lord. If you fail in this you must be born again to come back to earth to live your life all over. Through all of this Jesus remained silent. Caiaphas asked him if he denied these words and Jesus said no it is true. Do you also say we are all one with God and God lives within all of us. Jesus said I do not deny it.

Caiaphas arose from his chair looked at the priests, rabbis, and elders, the jury who would decide the fate of Jesus. A look of satisfaction shone on his face clearly showing the triumph he felt at this moment. Raising his hand to gain attention he said, "you have heard it how do you say? The jurors answered. "guilty." Let him suffer death. There was no discussion among them. the guilty verdict was decided before the trial began. The next morning the council met to approve the death warrant. Death by hanging on the cross. Jesus had been bound and led away the day before. The jailors had not fed him or even gave him water on orders of the high priest. With food in his stomach he might have vomited while on the cross which could have aroused sympathy among those in attendance.

One more step remained. According to Roman rule it was that Pilate himself refuse or approve the punishment. Caiaphas worried crucifixion might not be approved and this last part was important to end the threat of his teaching for once and all. Jesus was marched before the Roman leader who looked at him and said are you the one who calls himself the Son of God and says all are equal in the eyes of God? Jesus looked him in the eye and said yeah it is so. There is but one God and he resides in the heart of all of us. We are all children of Him and all are equal in His eyes so I say to you if God sees us as equals must we not do the same. Pilate said there is nothing I can do, take him away and do as you will.

Chapter Seventeen

Jesus was taken through the streets while crowds lined the way jeering and hurling vindictive at him. Many of those now calling out for his death were the ones who spent hours listening to his teaching. Some wept with compassion and prayed for his deliverance. A tourist named Simon had been pulled from the street by the soldiers and commanded to carry the cross, which he dragged on the ground as it was too heavy to carry.

Jesus walking with his hands bound, recalled the man he met back in India. The one who taught him how to go into his inner self, that part of you that is beyond the body where no one can hurt you. When pain is the worst he had said your heart will slow and almost stop. Perhaps he could stop the pain, but in his heart there was a pain caused by those who seemed out of control screaming for his death. Why had those who had called him rabbi and listened to his words now turn their back on him?

We stood along the way he must pass, tears welling up in our eyes, but when we looked there were tears in the eyes of Jesus himself. We knew they were out of pity for our suffering. Our mother, Mary Magdalene, James, Jude, Ruth, and myself shocked, none of us believed this could happen. "Perhaps he will be banished at the last moment, sent out of the country,but not hurt, we believed this totally."

We cried out to God to save him. We were unable to believe there would not be a last minute intervention by God. The lips of Jesus were moving as he looked at us. I knew he was praying for us. Finally in a place called Golgotha, meaning place of the skull they stopped. Here Simon the cross bearer was allowed to put down his burden and fled through the crowd, never to return to this place again. "They are barbarians he told himself."

My mother and Mary Magdalene told me to take Ruth and Jude away from this scene. Because of my identical appearance to Jesus she thought it was unsafe to remain here. Ruth and Jude could not bear to see what was going to happen. "Why do people do this to others and why does God allow this to happen?" Jude sobbed as I led them away. "We have total freedom to use our time on earth as we wish. God might influence us to do his will, but even then we may still follow our own dictates. It is when we leave our earthly bodies and return to heaven that we must judge ourselves and there is no harsher judge than that." I told him.

Jesus was fastened to the cross and it was lifted upright and dropped into a hole in the ground. It was the custom to break the legs of the criminals so they could not hold themselves upright and thus would die of suffocation because the weight of the body would collapse the lungs. For some reason I knew not why this was not done with Jesus so he held himself up using the footplate under his feet. Perhaps they thought death would be prolonged and more painful. Who knows? The hatred that had welled up since his arrest was beyond understanding.

The priests stood by pleased. It had all gone as planned. This threat to their power had been done away with. Those in the crowd who had brought lunches chose this moment to bring it out and ate while they waited for Jesus to die. Jesus prayed to God asking for his forgiveness and blessing. "My father he said forgive me my arrogance and know of my love." He heard the voice of God reply, "You have fulfilled my every wish and I am greatly pleased. I promise you will never need to come back to this earth again in human form." With that the head of Jesus slumped over and the crowd thinking he was dead began to leave. There was a great stillness in them as they slowly left the hill. Many wondered if they had done the wrong thing.

Later when everyone was gone except a few soldiers I came back and knelt at the foot of the cross weeping as I called out to him, "Jesus I love you so, and I do not want you to be gone." Then to my utter astonishment I heard Jesus speaking very quietly to me, "Thomas shed no tears, this is not over. I promise from all of this will come the pathway to save the world." I cannot explain how I felt at that moment, but before I could think further James appeared with some friends and said we have a place for his body, brother. Help us lift the cross and take him from it. With that we laid the cross flat and removed the nails that penetrated his body. We very gently carried him to a small cave that had been set aside as a tomb. Here we placed his body and all together moved a large stone over the entrance. The soldiers had followed us and their commander ordered two soldiers to stand guard and not allow anyone to enter. Then he said, "This is the least we can do for I feel a great wrong has been done today.

In that cold and damp cave the heart of Jesus began to slowly beat faster and life flowed through his body. God sent healing to stop the bleeding. After this Jesus heard the voice of God once more saying, "my son your work here is done, go far away and experience life as a human and have many years of happiness. Your life will never be forgotten and will be an example of how one should live on earth your memory will bring comfort for many in this world."

Later during the night the light of the moon became so brilliant it lit up the entrance to the cave and all around it. The brightness was so vivid it frightened the two guards who trembled in fear and ran away crying, "what have we done?" The heavy stone began to roll away on its own and Jesus walked out. As he left the cave Mary his mother and Mary Magdalene arrived drawn back to the site by a strong feeling they were unable to explain, Not expecting what they saw as the figure of Jesus walked out of the cave entrance. Shock, fear and confusion overtook them until slowly full realization filled them with joy. Jesus was alive.

Mary Magdalene rushed to pull his robe over him and as joy turned to concern they hurried him away lest others should appear. "This is truly the work of God" she said, "but you must flee immediately if they find you they will hack you to pieces." The way was slow as Jesus was very weak his legs trembling as he took each step. She led the little procession to a friend of hers where they told those inside it is Thomas the brother of Jesus who is ill we must tend to him. There they stayed until James found a donkey and cart and took Jesus home where he stayed until he was well enough to travel.

Mary Magdalene arranged for Jesus to meet with a group of disciples who could not believe this was real until Jesus showed his scars. "As you see I live, I have come from the grave, the power of the Lord God now calls you to take over my work. Carry on our work in all the areas we have discussed. Tell the truth as you know it to all people. The Holy Spirit is with you. Go, teach and heal for this you can do. I will go away and you will never see me again. You understand for me to stay will undo all we have worked for, the job is now yours. Never doubt you can do all I have done and more for you walk with the power of God working within you." Those disciples who were there later called all of the group together and made their plans. I travelled with Jesus and Mary Magdalene to the sea where I arranged for us to travel by boat to the far shore of a place now called Marseilles where we would be safe.

During this voyage Jesus and I wrote a book of his quotations. This you may know as the Gospel of Thomas. I took it with me when I left them and travelled east, eventually stopping in India. I never saw my brother and Mary again. I do know they found sanctuary in the land you now call France. Here they lived in peace where they had three children and many grandchildren. Jesus lived to be more than eighty years of age. God promised Jesus an opportunity to live as a normal human, to love, and grow old in the bosom of his family until he left his human body to go home Mary followed less than three years later… to Abba the Father.

EPILOGUE

When a fourteen year old boy asked for a teacher, God led him on a journey that lasted more than fourteen years. During that time he learned we here on earth are all joined together by one God. In each one of us there is a part of the Divine Spirit, no matter what that God is called or how that God is seen, when you say thank you it goes to one Divine Being. All beings no matter what part of this planet they are found, what colour of their skin, what language they speak, are united by where they came from as souls and where those souls will go back to when the journey on this planet is done.

That is what Jesus taught and that is why he was hung on a cross. The leaders of that time branded him a criminal because of his relentless insistence that we are all one under God. This is what doomed him. Thus Jesus would teach us today, to achieve global unity we need not all belong to the same religion, we need only to know that each of us finds the one and only God in our own way. We are united by having the same God within ourselves. We were born that way.

CPSIA information can be obtained at www.ICGtesting.com
Printed in the USA
LVOW07s0120030214

371855LV00001B/5/P